The Morning of America

The Morning of

The
Cultures
of
Mankind

THEODORE
K.
RABB,
Consulting
Editor

America, 1603-1789

*Darrett
B.
Rutman*

*The
University
of
New
Hampshire*

HOUGHTON

MIFFLIN

COMPANY

BOSTON
NEW YORK
ATLANTA
GENEVA, ILL.
DALLAS
PALO ALTO

OTHER BOOKS BY DARRETT B. RUTMAN

*The Old Dominion: Essays for Thomas
Perkins Abernethy* (edited, 1964)
*Winthrop's Boston: Portrait of a Puritan
Town, 1630–1649* (1965)
*Husbandmen of Plymouth: Farms and
Villages in the Old Colony,
1620–1692* (1967)
*American Puritanism: Faith and
Practice* (1970)
*The Great Awakening: Event and
Exegesis* (edited, 1970)

Printed in the U.S.A.

Library of Congress Catalog Card Number:
77–131289

ISBN: 0–395–04333–6

FOR
MORGAN
AND
ELIZABETH

Preface

THIS BOOK is for those interested in our origins as a nation. It is an introductory volume, one unabashedly proceeding from the assumption that the process by which an American nation was created is the essential (although by no means only) feature of the colonial and revolutionary periods of our history.

In writing the volume I have consciously "writ small," feeling that there is a certain intrinsic value in the quick overview. I have, for the most part, adopted a narrative style—this in the face of a modern tendency toward scientism with a concomitant display of methodology. The one deviation from this style—a short section on the process of Americanization—is meant to give the reader a position from which to contemplate the course of events as outlined in the narrative. I have, too fixed the focus of the volume upon the English colonies in North America which would eventually rebel and form the United States, ignoring the colonization efforts of other nations, even English colonization elsewhere in America. Broad comparative studies have their place, but the narrow focus engenders a clearer narrative when the subject is the appearance of the American nation. And I have eschewed the normal structure of colonial histories—the elaborate and detailed chronological discussion of the founding of each separate colony, two or three transitional chapters on social and intellectual history which are made to span the years from founding to revolutionary quarrel with Britain, a final elaborate and detailed chronological discussion of the Revolution and its aftermath.

This abandonment of the traditional structure was at first dictated by my desire to be brief. There was simply not enough room to discuss elaborately the coming of the various groups of colonists when, to my mind, other features of the century-and-a-half-plus of colonial existence were more important—the socio-political problems of the late seventeenth century, for example. I found, however, that the abandonment of the traditional structure freed me to wander in terms both of geography and time through the whole of the colonial experience, inquiring into characteristics essential to the period and to the nation to come. My hope is that the reader will both enjoy and profit from this freedom, and that, piqued by curiosity, he will read deeper on points which a volume of this scope can only suggest. Any pedagogical use of the volume might well be along just such lines: the volume to provide a quick survey of the period— the skeleton of data and trends which, in my own teaching, I have found students need if they are to avoid floundering; a variety of selected studies or primary materials to provide depth of detail and interpretation.

The volume has been in the making for several years, although not originally with the intent of its appearing in the present form. In various forms, consequently, the material and presentation have been commented upon by a number of friends, among them Norman K. Risjord of the University of Wisconsin, Robert V. Remini, of the University of Illinois at Chicago Circle, Kenneth A. Lockridge of the University of Michigan, Theodore K. Rabb of Princeton University, and John R. Howe, Jr., my former colleague at the University of Minnesota. I am indebted to each of them. And I am indebted—far more than is usually the case—to Daniel R. Sortwell of Houghton Mifflin Company who inspired the present form of the volume, patiently encouraged its completion, and so adeptly applied his editorial skills at various stages.

D.B.R.

Contents

Maps and Illustrations

The Morning of America

1.
Tudor Prelude

MARCH 24, 1603: Elizabeth, the last of England's Tudor monarchs, was gone! The virgin queen who had governed England for forty-five years, having nominated James Stuart of Scotland to be her successor and taken leave of her spiritual guardian, turned her face to the wall and quietly died. "The report of her death like a thunderclap was able to kill thousands," pamphleteer Thomas Dekker wrote, for Elizabeth's England was a nation that "was almost begotten and born under her"; her islanders had "never shouted any other *Ave* than for her name, never saw the face of any prince but herself, never understood what that strange, outlandish word *Change* signified." Dekker was a more grandiloquent than apt observer, however, for change had been a hallmark of Elizabeth's England, indeed of the whole Tudor period which had begun in 1485 with her grandfather, Henry VII (d. 1509).

The England of Henry VII had been a poor land, its economy revolving around subsistence agriculture and the export of wool and cloth, a land of provincial and town loyalties, an overbearing and turbulent nobility. Its foreign policy, inextricably bound up with the dynastic pretensions and aspirations of continental monarchs, sacrificed English interests to French, German, or Spanish. Its com-

1

merce had been dominated by foreigners. Its clerics had looked to Rome and the Pope for authority rather than to England's court and monarch.

In contrast, the England from which Elizabeth departed was a wealthy land, its economy quick, vibrant, multifacet-ed. There was much poverty: A steadily rising population had set in motion a complex series of economic shifts. In the countryside the relatively stable land structure of an earlier day was disrupted, and some men lost out and were turned off land which their families had operated for generations. Such losers had gravitated to the towns, swelling their populations, serving as a labor force in new commercial, manufacturing, and mining ventures. (London doubled in population during Elizabeth's reign.) But the towns could not absorb all of the labor released from agriculture and many of the dispossessed simply wandered as the unemployed "paupers" and "sturdy beggars." But there was opportunity as well, and for those who lost in the shifting economy there were others who gained: Men more quick witted or simply luckier could take advantage of the very instability which was impoverishing some to move ahead. Land was available in quantities unknown in England since the Norman conquest of five centuries before, while the growing towns provided enlarged markets for agricultural produce. "Sturdy yeomen," country gentlemen, and landed nobles found in larger markets better profits than ever before and prospered, even increasing their holdings by taking on more land. Such men were a more significant segment of society than the "sturdy beggars," although the literature of the time made more of the latter. Similarly, in the towns and particularly in London, the quickening economy was creating opportunity as goods and services were needed on an ever-larger scale. Opportunity spurred ambition, men "gaped" for gain, and a poet wrote of

> *Money, the minion, the spring of all joy;*
> *Money, the medicine that heals each annoy;*

Money, the jewel that man keeps in store;
Money, the idol that women adore!

The England from which Elizabeth departed was an England in which political authority had become centralized about the person and court of a monarch vitally concerned for English interests and revered as the head of a single, unified, English community. Pamphleteers and poets reflected the change in their passionate nationalism. John Lyly, writing in 1580, waxed eloquent about his queen: "O divine nature! O heavenly nobility! O fortunate England that hath such a Queen; ungrateful if thou pray not for her, wicked if thou do not love her, miserable if thou lose her." William Shakespeare, in his *Richard II,* was even more eloquent about his England:

> *. . . this scepter'd isle,*
> *This earth of majesty, this seat of Mars,*
> *This other Eden, demi-paradise;*
> *This fortress built by nature for herself*
> *Against infection and the hand of war;*
> *This happy breed of men, this little world,*
> *This precious stone set in the silver sea,*
> *Which serves it in the office of a wall,*
> *Or as a moat defensive to a house,*
> *Against the envy of less happier lands;*
> *This blessed plot, this earth, this realm,*
> *this England.*

The Tudor monarchs, in curbing the turbulence of the nobility and in building a strong and pervasive royal administration, contributed to the growth of nationalism. Economic forces played a part, too, most noticeably in breaking down the medieval localism of the towns. London, close by the seat of royal power, was rising to a towering place in the economic life of the kingdom and localism could not long exist in the face of the increasingly central position of "the City." Another push toward central government came from English merchants who needed a strong monarch to break the monopoly of foreign traders. But one can see a subtler transfer of allegiance from locality to nation. In that day the good of the community was held in greater esteem than was the free individual, and the economic behavior of the individual was circumscribed in the interest of the community. True, the situation was changing. The economic shifts were tending to unleash competition and free the individual. But ideals generally trail along after real life, changing slowly to reflect a changing reality. Hence men still insisted on extensive economic regulation to curb the individual on behalf of the community even while a new ideal of individualism was in the making. When their towns were incapable of controlling competition, townsmen turned to the higher authority of the nation, soliciting and obtaining economic legislation on a national scale. The higher authority was no more successful in resisting the slow trend toward economic individualism than the lower, but loyalty to the local community had been effectively abandoned in favor of loyalty to the larger community of all England.

Political centralism and nationalism were also intertwined with the Protestant Reformation which began on the continent early in the sixteenth century. Henry VIII (1509-1547) was England's king when Martin Luther let loose ideas which had been half-hidden for centuries in Europe and so set in motion the Reformation. And Henry was adamant against Luther, earning for his support of Catholicism the title *Fidei Defensor*—"Defender of the Faith." If he (and Englishmen in the main) defended the Catholic faith, however, neither king nor people was entirely happy with the Catholic Church in which that faith reposed. The Church's lands and wealth evoked envy. Its power, and the fact that its ultimate authority was the Pope in Rome, grated on Henry's aspirations for an England united under his sovereignty. Its financial exactions and temporal jurisdiction, the haughty attitude of its prelates, the many cases (real and imagined) of unworthy and uneducated priests, all bred anti-clericalism. Henry's matrimonial problem—one involving political and moral questions and not just Henry's lust for Anne Boleyn—precipitated the actual break, but it was not a hard wrench for England. Such an act had been in the making for years. Moreover, the break with the Catholic Church was not immediately followed by a break with the Catholic faith. Henry, rather than the Pope, was declared "Supreme Head" of Christ's church in England; neither the beliefs nor the structure of Christ's church was changed.

Nevertheless the effect was profound. On the surface the divorce from Rome divided England into Roman Catholics and Henrican- or Anglo-Catholics. Because Henry's actions were followed by an influx of radical Protestant ideas from the continent there were also those Englishmen who would go farther, effect changes in faith, and make England truly Protestant. Yet at the same time England became more united. Underlying the divorce from Rome was so radical a statement of political thought as to be called "revolutionary" by English historians. England was declared "an imperium" or "empire" in and of itself, a self-governing state free from any superior authority whether papal or feudal, legal or moral. All inhabitants of the realm were compacted together as a single community owing exclusive allegiance to a monarch possessing a divine grant to rule both the English church and the English state. There was no higher authority on earth than the English king—so most Englishmen believed in 1603.

Even those arch-Protestants who strove to push England ever farther along the road toward Luther and John Calvin (the second great Protestant leader of the continent) worked largely to convert monarch, church, and all England to their position rather than break the fabric of the single community united under the king. Their efforts were only partially successful. In the early years of Elizabeth's reign the break with Rome eventuated in the creation of no more than a partially reformed establishment. Many agonized over the incompleteness of the English reformation and, seeking a further "purification" of the church, earned for themselves the name "Puritan." Puritan ministers particularly urged changes in doctrine and ritual, even turning their attack on the very structure of episcopacy, the hierarchy of the church, arguing for an end to bishops and archbishops. Within their churches such ministers introduced radical reformed practices in contravention of legally established ways. But until well into the seventeenth century only an infinitesimal minority of the Puritans were driven by their beliefs to break the unity of the English community and, as so-called "Separatists," effect "reformation without tarrying" for the rest of England by establishing small, independent, and highly illegal churches of their own.

The separation from Rome was inevitably followed by a realignment of England's foreign policy. A traditional, dynastically-oriented alliance with Spain and hostility toward France were out of place in a world in which the Reformation was casting Catholic against Protestant in a European civil war. England, Protestant to the extent of being anti-papacy, tended to align with the Protestants of Germany and the Low Countries against the Catholic power of Spain and to support Protestant Frenchmen against Catholic Frenchmen in their wars of religion. But because the English monarch was never quite wealthy enough to plunge recklessly into war, because the Protestants everywhere seemed such weak reeds against the power of Spain, and because England was never thoroughly Protestant in faith, never approached the extremes of Luther or Calvin, the alliance with continental Protestants was never complete. The shift in foreign policy was, consequently, toward isolation and a cherishing of England's peculiar insularity. And this isolation, together with the very peculiarity of her religion—always only semi-Protestant—was very much an element of English national identity, one readily seen in the frequent allusions of the Elizabethan litterateurs to "the wooden walls of England" (the ships which guarded her coasts) and in Shakespeare's laudation of "this fortress built by nature for herself."

Vibrant and nationalistic: such was the England which Elizabeth departed in March 1603. And yet it was curiously tinged with melancholy. In part the melancholy grew from the fact that the great dreams of glory for England born of nationalism—those of Drake and Raleigh, for example, which we will note in passing—were never quite fulfilled. In part it was that the aspirations born of a vibrant economy could never be quite satisfied. But the melancholy went deeper. It was lodged in discomfort with the age itself and in an apparent contrast between ideals and discerned realities.

A particular ideal of man's proper relationship to his society prevailed in Elizabethan England, one rooted in a philosophic notion of the nature of man which was medieval and closely allied to religion. Man was not envisioned as a noble individual, as the nineteenth and to some extent the twentieth centuries tended to see him. He was, rather, a degenerate being, the seed of fallen Adam. He had joined together with other men in society for the protection, comfort, and guidance toward heaven that society could give him, and in so doing had obligated himself to serve the society in every way he could, sublimating his own degenerate urges in order that the society as a whole could prosper. Society itself was envisioned as an ordered and static chain of social existences extending from the laborer in the field to the king upon the throne. Within this chain—to paraphrase the English catechism of 1549— each individual was obligated to submit himself to all his governors, teachers, spiritual pastors, and masters, to order himself deferentially and reverently toward his betters, and to deal benevolently with all his inferiors. Further, he was to keep his body in temperance, soberness, and chastity, not to covet nor desire other men's goods nor positions, but to learn and labor truly to get his own living and to do his duty in whatsoever state of life God had placed him.

In a changing England these ideals, to some, seemed honored more in the breach than in the performance. Where was order in the face of change? Where was deference when "dunghill drudges" winning wealth in the economy "wax so proud that they will presume to wear on their feet what kings have worn on their heads"? Where was benevolence and the subordination of self to society when ambition provoked greed and avarice and the exploitation of one man by another? The disparity between the ideal of society and the discerned reality provoked discomfort, and discomfort was augmented by a religiosity spurred by the Reformation. Preachers called men to Christ-like lives in a time and place uncharitable to the meek and rewarding to the grasping. Men pulled alternately by Christ and Mammon—by their awesome sense of God's commands and their ambitions—despaired. "The earth," Shakespeare's Hamlet moaned, seemed but "a sterile promontory."

In Elizabeth's life, melancholia did not overtake a nationalistic optimism in England's destiny. And to the most vocal of Elizabethans that destiny was abroad. In this lies the last contrast between England at the ascension of Henry VII and at the death of Elizabeth. The earlier England was still medieval in its limited knowledge of the world; the latter England had begun to respond to the expansion of European horizons and to the discovery of new worlds across the Atlantic.

2.

England's Discovery of America

THE WORLD KNOWN to Englishmen of 1485—the year Henry VII came to the throne—and to Europeans in general at the time, was small and cramped. To the simple farmer the world was limited to his village and its surrounding fields, possibly the road to and from the nearest market town and the town itself. To the merchant or seaman the world was larger, but nevertheless confined to his own city or town, those with which he traded, and the routes between. Some, certainly the merchants and seamen of Italy, knew of India and the Far East as the ultimate source of spices and silks, or the Levant (the Mediterranean coast of the Near East) where the Venetians and Genoese bought finely wrought gold and silverware. To the learned scholar the world was larger still. Yet his knowledge was based on that of the ancient Greeks and Romans and was limited to Europe and those lands immediately bordering the Mediterranean and Black Seas—the classic tripartite world of Asia, Africa, and Europe. There was more to the world than this, of course, for the scholars knew that the world was a globe and gauged its approximate size. But what lay beyond the narrow limits of the known was filled with imaginative fantasy or equally imaginative theory. Just as the simple farmer filled what was unknown to him with trolls and leprechauns, devils and demons, the scholar filled the unknown world with boiling, impassable oceans and lands so torrid or so frigid as to forbid habitation by man.

The Chronology of Discovery

The expansion of Europe—of which the English settlement in America was but a small part—involved a widening of horizons and a dispelling of myth. As such it was a process of the mind as much as of ships sailing unknown seas, of scholars discovering in Ptolemy's *Geography* (a lost work of antiquity recovered and published in 1411) a better description of the world than they had before, as much as of Christopher Columbus, in 1492, entering the Caribbean in search of China. It was, moreover, a long process as knowledge trickled through societies from a few scholars and seamen to an ever-wider circle of courtiers and merchants, ultimately to the simple farmers and handicrafters who would become colonists.

The Mediterranean was the vital center of trade and commerce, art and literature, and learning. The widening of men's horizons began from there and was carried forward by the scholars and seamen of Europe's Atlantic coast. In the fifteenth century, Portuguese seamen moved south along the African continent and finally, in 1487, rounded the southernmost point and entered the Indian Ocean. In the sixteenth century, Spaniards following in the wake of Columbus explored the Caribbean, invaded and ransacked the Indian kingdoms of Central and South America. Frenchmen, following in the wake of Spaniards, probed the eastern coast of what would be the United States.

Knowledge of a wider world seeped slowly into an England on the outer edges of Europe; viewed from the

Mediterranean only Scotland, Ireland, Iceland, and Scandinavia were farther removed from the center. Henry VIII received instruction in the new geography through maps drawn for him by Spaniards, Italians, and Frenchmen, as did his daughter, the Princess Mary, from her Spanish tutor. A scholar here and there became cognizant of the expanded world: Ptolemy's *Geography* was available in Latin in England a century after its publication in Italy,

THE UNFOLDING WORLD OF THE FIFTEENTH AND SIXTEENTH CENTURIES

THE TRIPARTITE WORLD OF THE MEDIEVAL SCHOLAR
Redrawn from Antonio Ballestros Beretta:
GENESIS DEL DESCUBRIMIENTO

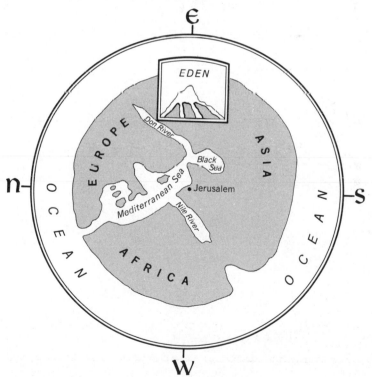

THE WORLD OF 1450
Adapted from Ptolemy's Geography

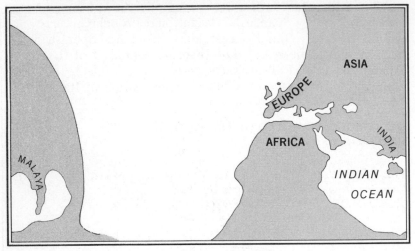

THE WORLD AS COLUMBUS ENVISIONED IT

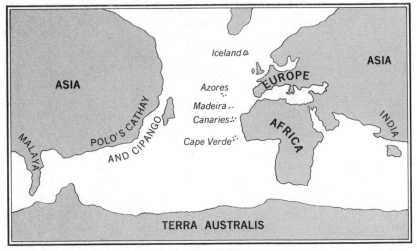

The World As John Cabot Envisioned It

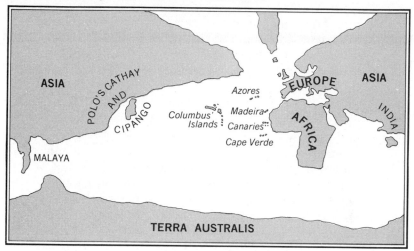

The World As The Elizabethans Envisioned It

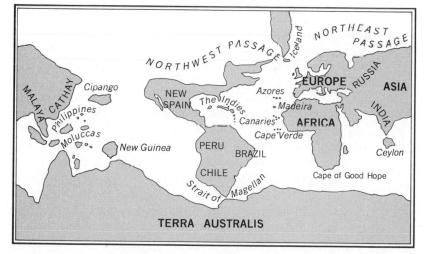

while Sir Thomas More reflected the very newest discoveries when he located his mythical *Utopia* of 1516 in the New World. And English seamen and merchants brought a practical knowledge to the kingdom. Even before the voyage of Columbus, probably as a result of rumors of land to the westward brought home by their ships trading in Ireland and Iceland, merchants from Bristol had sent a ship into the Atlantic in search of an unknown Atlantic island. In 1497 they backed John Cabot, a Venetian living in their town, as he sailed westward in the futile hope of finding a way to Japan and the Asian continent. In the years after, men from Bristol, Plymouth, and Southampton traded through Spain and Portugal to Africa, the Atlantic islands (the Azores, Madeira, Canaries, and Cape Verde), and with America, some even traveling to the New World aboard Spanish ships. By 1530 their trade with Spain and Portugal was significant enough to warrant a royal charter. That same year William Hawkins of Plymouth began trading in Brazil and along the West African coast, bringing home cargoes of dyewood, ivory, and pepper.

The England to which such men were bringing the knowledge and goods of an expanding world was, as we have noted, a changing land and in changing was becoming more and more receptive to that knowledge. One result of that series of economic shifts set in motion by a rising population was the accumulation of uncommitted capital, particularly, but not exclusively, in the hands of London merchants. As capital accumulated, funds were more readily available for overseas ventures, each prompted by the awareness of new lands and new trading opportunities, yet at the same time widening England's horizon to encompass still newer lands and opportunities. Thus in the 1550s Londoners inaugurated trades with the Moroccan coast, West Africa, and the Russian plains. In the 1560s they dreamed of opening an overland trade via Russia to India and China. Audacious as a group, however, the Londoners were necessarily cautious as individuals. Opening a new trade in a far corner of the world was an expensive and hazardous enterprise; no single merchant would gamble a sizeable part of his fortune. Hence the merchants evolved the joint-stock company, a device whereby each participant invested only a moderate sum and received a profit (or absorbed a loss) in proportion to the amount ventured. The investing merchants constituted, in a sense, a corporation. The most significant corporations received royal charters giving the group authority to establish and maintain by force, if necessary, a monopoly of whatever trade they were after. In 1555 a Russian Company was chartered, in 1577 a Cathay Company, in 1581 a Levant Company, in 1588 an African Company, in 1600 an East Indian Company. Ultimately the company would serve as a device to gather capital for American ventures.

Equally as important as the accumulation of capital was the emergence during the sixteenth century of that strident, vociferous English nationalism we have mentioned. For while cautious isolationism was a watchword of foreign policy and insularity an element of English nationalism, nationalistic Englishmen nevertheless entered the Protestant-Catholic fray, streaming out of their island fortress to fight for God, country, queen, and booty. Men like Walter Raleigh, Richard Grenville, Martin Frobisher, and Humphrey Gilbert fought in the tangled wars of Hungary (between Protestants, Catholics, and Turks), in Ireland, France, and the Low Countries. They took to sea to seize Spanish ships and, like Francis Drake, raid Spain's Caribbean settlements. Their involvement abroad led to dreams of expansion. Thus Grenville schemed to take possession for England of a much-rumored "Terra Australis" or "Southern Land" thought to stretch south and west from the Straits of Magellan. Drake sought to build an English empire by taking over the Portuguese possessions after Spain, in 1580, gobbled up her neighbor on the Iberian peninsula and sent the Portuguese pretender into English exile. Drake argued, at least let England seize the Portuguese Azores as a base from which to raid the treasure fleets sailing from Mexico and Panama to Spain. English eyes were on the New World, the source of Spanish wealth. They would have England seize and occupy a part of it, or at least establish bases for raiding the Spanish Caribbean and from which a search could be made for a route across or through the continent to the Pacific and the Orient. In 1578 and 1583 Gilbert sought to establish a colony far to the north in Newfoundland, but lost his life in the attempt. His younger half-brother, Raleigh, pushed forward the project, shifting his effort southward to what he called "Virginia" in honor of his virgin queen. In 1585, 1586, and 1587 settlers were left on Roanoke Island off the coast of present-day North Carolina. The first group shipped home aboard an English fleet which stopped off on its return from Caribbean raiding. The second and third simply disappeared.

As her merchants and venturers turned abroad, England's knowledge of the world slowly grew. English knowledge was still so scant in the 1550s that the earliest London voyages were of necessity guided by Portuguese, French, and Spanish pilots and were largely planned by John Cabot's son, Sebastian, who had served Spain for thirty-five years prior to returning to England in 1548. Indeed, a voyager of the 1560s, sailing without a foreign pilot, attempted to make Cuba from the north coast of South America but missed the island completely and made land on the Florida coast. As late as Gilbert's and Raleigh's voyaging, foreign pilots were still utilized. But Englishmen learned from their pilots, by experience, and from each other, the reports of each voyage circulating widely. And they learned more formally from scholars and publicists.

John Dee was one such scholar. Having gone abroad "to speak and confer with some learned men" and to study at Louvain and Paris, he returned to England in 1551 a skilled geographer, mathematician, and a master of medieval travels in Asia. For thirty years he listened to returning voyagers, mapped their discoveries, speculated on how to fit what each had learned into a coordinate view of the whole globe, and advised new voyagers on how to proceed. Richard Eden, a Cambridge scholar and government servant, translated and, in 1553, published portions of a German geography dealing with the earliest Spanish discoveries. In 1555 appeared his *Decades of the New World*, a miscellany which included accounts of English and foreign voyaging, a discourse on metals, and a Dutch treatise on the measurement of longitude. Perhaps his most significant work appeared in 1561, a translation of Martin Cortes' *Arte of Navigation*, the official handbook of the Spanish pilots. Regularly reprinted throughout the rest of the century, it guided English seamen across the world. Another scholar was Richard Hakluyt, a lawyer whose dealings with London merchants brought him into contact with their widening world. By the 1570s he was an accepted authority on English trade throughout the world, advising merchants on trade with Turkey, Persia, the possibilities of a northeast passage to Asia, and what to expect in the Americas. More important than any, however, was Hakluyt's nephew, Richard Hakluyt the Younger.

Uncle introduced nephew to geography, the younger Hakluyt himself describing in a letter the scene when, as a schoolboy, he visited the elder's rooms in London. Maps and books were strewn about, and the uncle, seeing the boy "somewhat curious," began "to instruct his ignorance," explaining "the division of the earth into three parts after the old account, and then according to the later, and better distribution, into more." On a map he pointed "to all the known Seas, Gulfs, Bays, Straights, Capes, Rivers, Empires, Kingdoms, Dukedoms, and Territories of each part" of the globe "with declaration also of their special commodities, and particular wants, which by the benefit of traffic, and intercourse of merchants, are so plentifully supplied." The discourse so enthralled the youth that he determined to make the pursuit of geographic knowledge his life's work. At Oxford he "read over whatsoever printed or written discoveries and voyages" he "found extant either in the Greek, Latin, Italian,

Spanish, Portugal, French, or English languages" and began lecturing on the new geography. In Paris with an English embassy he broadened his knowledge. Back in
England he mingled "with the chiefest Captains at sea,
the greatest Merchants, and the best Mariners of our nation," collecting their accounts of voyages and descrip-
tions of far-off lands. These he published in a number of
works, most notably his *Divers Voyages, Touching the Dis-
coverie of America, and the Ilands Adjacent*... of 1582
and *The Principall Navigations, Voiages and Discoveries
of the English Nation* which appeared in 1589, and, in a
much expanded edition, in 1598–1600.

Hakluyt's "chiefest Captains at sea," together with the
merchants who invested in overseas enterprises and scholars and publicists such as Hakluyt himself, constituted a
small but ardent group, devoted to the idea of a "greater
England." Knowledgeable of the widening world, they
found their tight little island too small. They would have
Englishmen strike out in all directions—northeast, northwest, through the Straits of Magellan or around the Cape
of Good Hope, to India, Asia, Terra Australis, or the New
World. They would conquer or colonize Ireland, or Newfoundland, or Virginia. They would fight Catholic Spain at
sea, in the Netherlands, or in Spain itself and so make the
world safe for their Protestant God. They would enrich
England by expanding her trade. And within the limits of
a cautious policy, their queen helped them. She invested
in their endeavors and lent them ships from the royal
navy. She chartered the merchants' companies and authorized first Gilbert, then Raleigh, to discover and take
possession of New World lands not claimed by any other
Christian monarch, to exercise absolute authority over
such lands and enjoy what profit they could make. She
honored her seamen—knighting Sir Francis Drake for example. But she curbed their activities, too, particularly as
the 1580s advanced and formal war with Spain broke out.
Invasion threatened, was attempted (the Spanish Armada
of 1588), then threatened again, and the queen kept her

captains close to England to defend her shores. The schemes and plans of the greater England men, their dreams of a world-wide English power, of English colonies and trading posts, were held in abeyance until Elizabeth's death, the accession of James Stuart and, in 1604, peace with Spain.

The America of the Mind

To the greater England men the world was, as one historian has written, "an oyster to be opened by the sword." The American continents were only a part of this world. But the Americas, far more than the Russian plains, or Africa, or India, caught the imagination of Englishmen in the latter sixteenth and early seventeenth centuries. In pamphlets, plays, and poems Englishmen read of the New World; more importantly, they talked of the Americas, passing facts and fancies by word of mouth. One cannot say that the news of America swept England from end to end. The average Englishman had many more important things on his mind. But it did trickle from the greater England men of the court and counting-house and deep-sea wharf to an ever-broader circle in London and other ports, eventually to country houses and villages in the English shires. And the knowledge prompted some men to try their mettle in the New World, bold venturesome men at first, more stolid and mundane men later. What promises did the New World offer them, the venturesome and the stolid? What view of America tempted them to hazard themselves, eventually their families, in a wilderness?

Those Englishmen who were first aware of the New World saw it through Spanish eyes. The New World was the Indies, the Caribbean, New Spain (Mexico), the Spanish Main (the north coast of South America), and Peru. It was a warm and languid land, rich in tropic fruits and, of course, gold and silver. In Sir Thomas More's *Utopia*, gold and silver were so plentiful as to be despised by the natives who made of them chamber pots "and other like vessels that serve for most vile uses." In the Spanish ac-

counts of the New World incorporated into Richard
Eden's *Decades of the New World*, Peru boasted silver,
pearls, precious stones, spices, and so much gold that the
inhabitants "make pisspots thereof"; along the Spanish
Main gold and pearl ornaments were as common among
women as glass ornaments among the women of Spain;
New Spain had great cities with paved streets, magnificent temples, and marvelously wrought gold and silver
work; the Caribbean was sprinkled with verdant islands,
gold-laden and fruitful, where men lived richly, without
great labor. That such accounts were not exaggerated
seemed clear as English captains plundered the Caribbean
and seized treasure ships on their way to Spain. Home
again, the captains were lionized. The stories of their
deeds and profits circulated in the seaports and in London, gaining with retelling. Publicists and poets, friends of
men such as Drake and Raleigh, presented in print the
vision of a golden New World. Playwrights trumpeted the
wealth of the Indies to young gentlemen crowding the
cockpits of the Southwark theaters across Thames River
from London. For example, Christopher Marlowe's dying
hero of *Tamburlaine* (1586) calls for a world map and tells
his sons:

> *Look here my boys, see what a world of ground*
> *Lies westward from the midst of* Cancer's *line. . . .*
> *And shall I die, and this unconquered?*
> *Lo here my sons, are all the golden mines,*
> *Inestimable drugs and precious stones,*
> *More worth than* Asia, *and the world beside.*

When the captains summoned these young gentlemen
to venture with them in search of "new worlds, for gold,
for praise, for glory," some of the gentlemen responded—
the "young heir or cockney" described by pamphleteer
Thomas Nash, "that is his mother's darling" and has
"played the waste-good at the Inns of the Court or about
London." He "falls in a quarreling humor with his fortune,

because she made him not King of the Indies, and swears and stares, after ten in the hundred, that ne'er such a peasant as his father or brother shall keep him under: he will to sea, and tear the gold out of the Spaniards' throats."

Englishmen saw the New World, too, through eyes entranced by medieval legend. The medieval mind had sprinkled the Atlantic with mythical islands, all boasting perfect societies. Why not then find perfection in America —the legendary Cibola, or the Fountain of Youth, by extrapolation from the Bible the land of Ophir, perhaps Eden itself? Perfection and riches were combined in More's *Utopia*, which was not only a gold-laden land but a perfect commonwealth. The societies of the American Indians were at first seen in this light. The Indians were, in Eden's *Decades*, "simple souls," the "most happy of all men." Having no skill in deceit, they had no need of "weights and measures"; they had no use for "pestiferous money, the seed of innumerable mischiefs." "They seem to live in that golden world of which old writers speak so much: wherein men lived simply and innocently without enforcement of laws, without quarreling judges and libels, content only to satisfy nature"—phrases which imply as much about the author's melancholy view of his contemporary England as they do about his image of America. In Hakluyt's work, the Indians were "most gentle, loving and faithful, void of all guile and treason, and such as live after the manner of the golden age." (Only subsequently would actual settlement produce an opposite image—that of the Indian as savage, brutish, hostile, and treacherous.) The notion of perfection also encompassed the idea of the perfectibility of the Englishmen in the new lands. The lush riches of America, its idyllic qualities—Eden-like—would by some subtle alchemy transform sloth to diligence, vice to virtue; the trollop would find chastity, the fop industry, the ostentatious frugality. Even the criminal would be regenerated. Those who, "for trifles may otherwise be devoured by the gallows," "the wandering beggars of England, that grow up idly, and hurtful and burdenous to this

realm, may there be unladen, better bred up" to the benefit of their country "and to their own more happy state."
It was a constant refrain, despite the objections of some
few that nothing good could be made of "the scum of
people and wicked condemned men." The very air of the
New World was put forth as therapeutic, and "many that
have been weak and sickly in old England," by journeying
overseas, could be "thoroughly healed and grown health-
ful strong."

In this atmosphere it is not surprising that some men
would make the leap from personal rejuvenation to a
broader vision: the perfectibility of society as a whole. The
New World was in a natural state, untouched, devoid of
institutions, a clean slate on which men could attempt to
draw anew and more perfectly the outlines of human society. Here was "nature in its beautiful simplicity, as it
came from the hands of its creator; without having been
altered or depraved by ambition or art." One could so
easily muse with Shakespeare's Gonzalo in *The Tempest*
(1603):

> *Had I plantation of this isle, my lord,—...*
> *And were the King on't, what would I do?*

and conjure one's own utopia.

The promise of perfection commingled always with a
promise of riches in the English mind, although exactly
what constituted riches changed in time. Some Englishmen might set to sea to tear gold out of Spanish throats
and enrich themselves and their nation. But those who
thought of more substantial activity than freebooting were
faced with a cardinal tenet of medieval science. Precious
metals and stones were produced, it was thought, by the
heat of the sun and hence were to be found in greatest
quantities at the equator. The farther north or south one
went, the less likelihood there was of gold and silver.
Spain occupied the Caribbean and claimed equatorial
America; Spanish power, together with Elizabeth's cau-

tious policy, forbade most attempts to exploit directly any land other than the northern coast along which John Cabot had sailed. But along that northern coast there were "no riches of gold, spices, nor precious stones," wrote Robert Barlowe in the 1540s, "for it stands far apart from the equinoctial whereas the influence of the sun does nourish and bring forth gold, spices, stones and pearls." A discovery of gold in the far north in 1576 seemed incredible, a contravention of the natural law, and excitement ran high among the greater England men; the truth—that the gold was only pyrite or fool's gold—was all the more disappointing.

Gold would remain a part of the imagery of America. Sir Walter Raleigh, in the 1590s and again in 1617, sought along the Orinoco River and Guiana coast for the fabled city of Manoa and El Dorado, its Indian king who rolled in gold dust every morning and washed it away each evening. Returning from his first voyage he wrote of Indian nobles powdered with gold and of a crystal mountain from which Indians gathered diamonds. Playwright George Chapman, a friend of Raleigh, in *Eastward Hoe* (1605) had one character, Seagull, exclaim in vigorous Elizabethan English: "Come, boys, Virginia longs till we share the rest of her maidenhead. . . .

I tell thee, gold is more plentiful there than copper is with us. . . . Why, man, all their dripping-pans and their chamber-pots are pure gold; and all the chains with which they chain up their streets are massy gold; all the prisoners they take are fettered in gold; and for rubies and diamonds,they go forth on holidays and gather them by the seashore.

Gold fever would grip the first settlers of Virginia when, in 1608, the discovery of what one called "gilded dirt" led to a period of "no talk, no hope, no work, but dig gold, wash gold, refine gold, load gold." And as late as 1619, in his ode to *The Virginian Voyage*, Michael Drayton would send Britons forth "to get the pearl and gold and ours to hold *Virginia*, earth's only paradise." Nevertheless, the promised riches of the New World were, for Englishmen, shifting.

Men like the Hakluyts began the change. Less interested in gold and more in trade, they dreamed of a stable, English-controlled market for English wool and of purely English sources for the silk, dyes, drugs, and tropical products that came to England from Spain, Italy, and France, and for the tar, pitch, cordage, planking and spars which came from the Baltic area. As English nationalists they objected to enriching enemies and "doubtful friends" by trading with them. As embryonic economists they feared that England's trade, linked so firmly to the continent, could be easily cut off and England strangled, and they generally thought of any imports from the continent as a drain on England's "treasure." Thus, in 1578, the elder Hakluyt drew up a set of notes to guide English efforts in the New World. What was to be sought, he wrote, was a land with a climate similar to that of Spain or southern France, "temperate" and "sweet," that it might be occupied and utilized in such a way as to end England's dependence "upon Spain for oils, sacks [sherry], raisins, oranges, lemons, Spanish skins, etc ... upon France for wood, basalt, and Gascony wines ... on Eastland [the Baltic area] for flax, pitch, tar, masts." To produce such goods for shipment to England, Englishmen would have to transport themselves overseas, not just to raid but to live with wives and families. A hundred settlers or so, carefully planted in the New World, would grow "in time" and "such league and intercourse may arise" as few yet dreamed, the elder wrote. Six years later the younger Hakluyt presented the same arguments in a "Discourse on the Western Planting" presented to the queen. But being closer to the ardently nationalistic and Protestant seamen than his uncle (who was closer to the merchants among the greater England men), the younger added that a New World settlement would be a convenient base for raiding the Caribbean, that it would "stay the Spanish king from flowing over all the face of that waste firmament," "abate the pride of Spain and of the supporters of the great Anti-Christ of Rome," and "enlarge the glory of the gospel, and from England plant sincere religion." How easy it would be, the young man wrote, for England swarmed with "valiant youths, rusting and hurtful by lack of employment." Let them, therefore, "be lords of all those seas."

The Hakluyts and those who, like them, advised such a course were not rash men offering a reckless scheme, although the younger Hakluyt was always more enthusiastic than the others. The idea of transplanting Englishmen to an alien environment was not new. In the 1560s it had been attempted in Ireland—a land then only a little less strange to Englishmen than was the New World—and by many of the same men involved in overseas expansion. The advocates of New World colonization had, moreover, read most if not all that had been written about the New World and carefully interviewed those returning from the voyages. But their knowledge was largely of Spanish America while their plans had to be effected on the northern coast. They had little detailed knowledge of the latter, Eden writing of it as "yet known but only by the sea coasts," a 1616 writer describing the New England shore as "still but even as a coast unknown and undiscovered." The proponents of colonies covered their ignorance with *a priori* reasoning, as in the matter of climate. It was, they said, perfectly clear that places of like degree of latitude on the globe, being equidistant from the equator, should have like climates; that, for example, the climate and hence products of Newfoundland would be similar to the climate and products of Paris, and the coast southward from Newfoundland as temperate as the Bay of Biscay and Iberia. And they were prone to suggest that whatever England needed the New World—specifically England's part of the New World—could produce, be it lemons or pomegranates, wines, silks, or shipstores. "Between the degrees of 30. and 60. of septentrional latitude," one proponent of colonies wrote, "by computations astronomical and cosmographical, are doubtless to be found all things that be necessary, profitable, or delectable."

Those who sailed for Gilbert or Raleigh, as English colonies were first attempted in America in the 1580s, did not disabuse the theorists at home, for the venturers tended to see in the New World what they expected to see. True, the northern part of Newfoundland was inexplicably cold, Edward Hayes wrote in describing the area of Gilbert's attempt. But "it cannot stand with reason and nature of the clime that the south parts should be so intemperate as the [rumor] hath gone" inasmuch as it "do lie under the climates of Briton, Anjou, Poictou in France." And more important than the climate were the "incredible quantity" and "variety" of fish, the "pitch, tar, soapashes, dealboard, masts for ships, hides, furs, flax, hemp, corn, cordage, linencloth, metals and many more . . . which the countries will afford, and the soil is apt to yield," the "roses passing sweet, like unto our musk roses in form," the raspberries fat and sweet, and the grasses which "fatten sheep in very short space." Subsequently he was to write of the Maine coast as having "like heat as Lisbon in Portugal," a "fair and pleasant" land which would "yield unto us besides wines and oils and sugars, oranges, lemons, figs, raisins, almonds, pomegranates, rice, raw silks such as come from Granada, and divers commodities for dyers, as anile and cochineal." Raleigh's attempt to establish a colony to the south on Roanoke Island was a failure but the emerging image of America did not suffer. His first voyagers to the coast in 1584 reported that they sensed their landfall by a fragrance "so sweet, and so strong . . . as if we had been in the midst of some delicate garden abounding with all kind of odiferous flowers." To Thomas Hariot, writing of his Roanoke Island sojourn in a *Brief and True Report of the New Found Land of Virginia* (1588), the air along the coast was "temperate and wholesome," the soil "fertile," and the products to be had included silk, flax, hemp, pitch, tar, rosin, turpentine, medicinal barks, wines, furs, iron, copper, pearls, dyes, sugar, oranges, lemons, and quinces. Inland America promised even more. Exploring settlers found "the soil richer, the trees taller, the ground firmer and the topsoil deeper"; "from the nature of the climate we gather that the land is similar to Japan, China, Persia, Jerusalem, the Islands of Cyprus and Candy, the southern parts of Greece, Italy, and Spain, and other famous countries."

For the most part, tracts and pamphlets such as Hariot's emanated from the small, interconnected group of greater England men. They were meant to convince the monarch and the great officers of state of the desirability of colonies, prospective investors of the profits to be had, and to offer tentative programs by which colonies might be developed. There was no conscious attempt to educate all England to the New World or to recruit ordinary men and women as colonists. There was no need to, for the writers thought in terms of gentlemen leaders—the same sort of venturesome and daring men who sailed with the sea captains—and a commonality taken from among the condemned and poor of England. But if not intended to educate, the pamphlet literature had that effect. A view of the Americas rich in commodities of all sorts came to overlie the initial image of a languid, gold-and-silver-rich land and the two imperceptibly merged—inasmuch as gold and silver were quick and easy ways to wealth, so too the commodities. By the time of Elizabeth's death the America of the mind was an easy land where riches of every sort could be had with little effort. Those who, with this image in mind, sailed to settle in Virginia and New England in the years immediately after 1603 were doomed to disappointment.

English America was, in reality, neither a rich nor an easy land. With hindsight we can see the attributes of the eastern seaboard which made colonization relatively easy. A low lying land, its great mountain chains were comfortably distant in the interior; not for 150 years would settlers be required to cross the mountains. The many bays and inlets afforded safe harbors and protected waterways— Chesapeake Bay, Delaware Bay, Long Island Sound, Narragansett Bay, Cape Cod Bay, Massachusetts Bay. Broad, navigable rivers—the Connecticut, Hudson, Delaware,

Potomac, Rappahannock, and James—formed "highways" into the interior. Settlements would cluster around these bays and rivers. Moreover, the soil of the seaboard, thin and quickly depleted, was nevertheless virgin and for a time richly abundant in English grains and vegetables. In neither flora nor fauna did English America differ radically from England and western Europe. Even the climates of the eastern coast of North America and northwestern Europe were roughly the same. Such similarities would make the adjustment from old to New World all the easier. Where flora and fauna did differ dramatically was largely in quantity. The abundance of game, fish, natural foods such as berries and wild grapes stood out in English minds, not the differences between particular American and English animals, fish, or wild foods—Indian corn being the one significant exception. Similarly, England knew the pine tree but not the extensive pine forests of the coast which would provide the wood to build and heat houses, construct fences and ships. Fate was kind, too, in that the forests were spotted with natural meadows and areas burned over by the Indians as they cleared land for planting. Most of the early settlements would be set down on such cleared land, easing the task of the colonists. Only after settlement was well underway would Englishmen face the heavy work of clearing the forests. The nature of the Indian population was an asset, for scattered thinly along the coast in small groups and lacking both the weapons and the unity necessary for warfare in European terms, the seaboard Indians seldom constituted a real threat to the English. Even the broad Atlantic which had to be crossed by the colonists was, in hindsight, an asset for it insulated the colonists from European wars and disturbances and allowed them to develop largely on their own.

Yet these attributes can be overstated. To the first English settlers the Atlantic was a fearsome moat separating them from home. One readily envisions the Roanoke settlers, or later those of Jamestown, gazing after the departing ships which had brought them from England, then turning to their encampment where, as one wrote, there was "neither tavern, beer-house, nor place of relief but the common kettle." The wilderness about them was a place to be explored, yet feared. In their writings one catches glimpses of the earliest settlers gamboling about the countryside one moment, gaily giving names to newly discovered cliffs, streams, lakes, but standing off a wolf with a stick of wood the next. The Indians, so weak and thinly scattered, were felt by the settlers to be a constant menace. The abundance of the wilderness was frequently above their ability to harvest. And the minor climatic differences were far more important than the similarities— the hot summers and bitterly cold and snowy winters of New England, the sultry, killing Virginia summers, the sudden, tempestuous rainfalls separated by days and weeks of burning sun, so unlike the frequent soft rains of England. Above all, however, the soil had to be worked to produce and the image of America of the first settlers was of production without work, or at least with minimal labor.

The view of an America rich in exotic possibilities would remain to tantalize Englishmen. Every burst of colonizing activity in the seventeenth and eighteenth centuries would be accompanied by ecstatic commentaries on the commodities to be obtained—a list which seldom varied. In 1717, for example, *A Discourse Concerning the Designed Establishment of a New Colony to the South of Carolina in the Most Delightful Country of the Universe* promised "coffee, tea, figs, raisins, currants, almonds, olives, silk, wine, cochineal, and a great variety of still more rich commodities which we are forced to buy at mighty rates from countries lying in the very latitude of our Plantation." Even the idea of easy opportunity was clung to, the same pamphlet promising "such easy benefits as will without the smallest waiting for the growth of plants be offered to our industry from the spontaneous wealth which overruns the country."

But a new image of America—a companion image—was

formed out of the disappointments of the first settlers. One senses it in the sublimation of the exotic in pamphlets and letters from colonists, and in their praise of commonplace achievements. Thus Ralph Hamor, writing from Virginia in 1614, paid but scant attention to "the relation of the Country commodities, which every former treatise has abundantly" considered; more important to him were the number of cattle, sheep, pigs, and acres in cultivation in Virginia. One senses the new image in an increasing caution in the description of the new land. "I will not do ... as some have done to my knowledge, speak more than is true," a pamphleteer of the post-settlement period wrote: "I will not tell you that you may smell the corn fields before you see the land; neither must men think that corn does grow naturally (or on trees) nor will the deer come when they are called." And one senses it in an honest acceptance of the difficulties of the New World. True, the soil was somewhat thin and weak in certain areas, but "if any man doubt of the goodness of the ground, let him comfort himself with the cheapness of it." True, too, the climate was different from England's. But the newcomer, by taking care the first year, could become acclimatized to Virginia's humid summers, and if the winters were longer and colder in New England there was nevertheless "wood good store, and better cheap to build warm houses, and make good fires, which makes the winter less tedious"; or, more tersely put, "here is good living for those that love good fires." Still another wrote "to discourage such as with too great lightness" decided on America. Those dazzled by the possibilities must realize, he wrote, that "as he shall have no rent to pay [for a house], so he must build his house before he have it," that as there was plenty of free wood in the forest, he must first "cut and fetch it home" before he burns it. The irresponsible writers who talked of the goodness of the New World and not of the labor it required were, the author charged, responsible for many failures for they tempted men unworthy of the task of settlement. "Can any be so simple as to conceive that the fountains would stream forth wine, beer, or the woods and rivers be like butchers' shops, or fishmongers' stalls, where they might have things taken to their hands? If thou canst not live without such things... rest where thou art."

America was still envisioned in terms of promise, but the promise was to the diligent rather than to the adventuresome. The land itself was the New World's greatest attribute, wanting only men and women to plant and reap. Writer after writer stressed the point during the years following actual settlement. "Pity it was, and is, to see so many goodly fields, and so well seated, without men to dress and manure the same." "The land affords void ground enough to receive more people than this state can spare, and that not only wood grounds, and others, which are unfit for present use; but in many places much cleared land for tillage, and large marshes for hay and feeding cattle." "The great quantity of corn ground impaled, [would be] sufficient if there were no more in the colony secured, to maintain with but easy manuring and husbandry, more men, than I suppose, will be addressed thither, (the more is the pity) these three years." Life was not easy. "I would have no man... trusting too much to the fertility of the bounds where he is to go, and too little to his own providence and industry." But for those who would labor on the land, the reward, if not rich, was complete. "Such as either through crosses in this world, or ... rents, or else great charge of children and family live here [in England] and that not without much care and sweat, into extreme poverty: for those," Hamor wrote, "this Country has present remedy." For "who can desire more content," wrote another, "that has small means or only his merit to advance his fortune, than to reap and plant the ground he has purchased by the hazard of his life? If he has but the taste of virtue and magnanimity, what to such a mind can be more pleasant, than planting and building a foundation for his posterity, got from the rude earth, by God's blessings and his own industry."

The Response to America

America as a gold-rich land, or as an easy land of exotic possibilities, appealed to the imaginative, the venturesome, the nationalistic, and to theorists such as the Hakluyts. It underlay the beginnings of English colonization as, in the years immediately after Elizabeth's death, the greater England men inspired an American venture. In 1607 outposts were established on James River in Virginia and on the Sagadahoc River (now the Kennebec) on the Maine coast. Sagadahoc was abandoned the next year; Jamestown, although continuing its existence, was singularly unsuccessful through its first decade. The years were experimental years during which a variety of governmental and economic organizations were attempted and the colonists were required by their English backers to try first one, then another commodity—wine, glass, iron, silk —in an almost frantic search for something of value which could be produced and shipped home. The first colonists themselves were no more than adventurers, looking for excitement, glory for their nation and themselves, and ultimately a quick personal profit. Too many were young gentlemen deluded by an image of America as a land of abundant and easy riches; too many thought of themselves as mere transients in the wilderness and intended to return to England once their fortunes were made. They argued with one another, shirked work, ran after fantasies— as when fool's gold was discovered. They died of fevers and, having antagonized the local Indians within weeks of their arrival, of Indian arrows as well. As one man deeply involved in the thrust to America wrote: "There must go other manner of spirits to settle this business, before it will be brought to pass."

England had "other manner of spirits." We have seen how, in country and town, the economic structure was in flux, and how some men bemoaned the changes they discerned. They thought of their England as diseased and contrasted it with an idealization of society in which men devoted themselves to their community and were content

in their natural places in a stable world, be their place
ploughboy or merchant prince, footman or duke. For such,
the image of America as virgin, inducive of the perfectibility of man, offered a new beginning, an opportunity to
effect social perfection. Along the same lines, one can add,
the New World appealed to the religiously disconsolate
Puritans uncomfortable in England's half-way reformation
and despairing of all efforts to transform the English
church. For such, the New World offered an opportunity
to serve their God in what they considered a more proper
fashion without disturbing the unity of the English community. The two groups—those dreaming of social perfection in the New World and those dreaming of religious
perfection—were sometimes synonymous, social perfection being easily defined in terms of doing God's bidding
here on earth.

Above all, however, the image of an America promising
opportunity for the diligent and hardworking appealed to
men and women caught up in the competition of the English economy. The appeal was not to those defeated by
the economy—the destitute beggars who wandered the
English countryside in the main tended to accept their
defeat—although to some extent the poor would be sent.
Wandering children would be swept from London's
streets and packed overseas; petty criminals, most often
from among the poor, would be given their choice of the
gallows or transportation. Neither was the appeal to those
benefiting most in the economy; the successful would not
hazard their success. The appeal was, rather, to the "middling sort," the farmer who had amassed some land but
was impatient for more, or his sons and daughters who had
tasted of their father's well-being and wanted their own,
or the petty shopkeeper of London anxious for quicker
advancement than he was making. Such men, if they
heard tales of gold in America or of an easy, languid life,
would only cluck their tongues in amazement and turn
back to work; the tales were so alien to their everyday
lives as to be all but meaningless. But hearing of America

in familiar terms—as a land of opportunity for farmers, craftsmen, tradesmen—they would accept it as a viable alternative to England, just as a Berkshire carpenter would accept the fact that there was work waiting in London, or an Essex farmer that there was land to lease in Sussex. The importunings of a colonial promoter, the departure of a friend or relative, the impetus of religion, or a dip in the economy making success all the more elusive in England, would tip the balance for some and they would go, quietly and without great fanfare, unconscious, as one historian has commented, "that they were doing anything remarkable." From any given town or village their numbers were few. One must always remember that no matter how many left, more stayed behind. But in the aggregate a flood of people began leaving England. From 1618 through the early 1640s, the period of what has been called "the great migration," more than 50,000 departed for Virginia, Bermuda, New England, Maryland, and, once England broke the Spanish monopoly of the Caribbean, to various Caribbean islands. Fully committed to the New World, as the gentlemen of Jamestown had not been, these thousands began the process of becoming something other than Englishmen.

3.

Colonization and Americanization

ENGLAND'S continental colonies, those which would eventually rebel and form the embryo of the United States, were laid down over the course of more than a century. Jamestown was settled in 1607 under the auspices of greater England men organized (in 1609) as the Virginia Company of London. From 1609 to 1616 Virginia had the air of a great national cause as merchants, London tradesmen, and prosperous country gentlemen invested money and hope in the colony. But during these early, experimental years returns were scant. English enthusiasm slackened. The colony rooted slowly, although by the early 1620s it was well enough established to withstand the fury of a massive and concerted Indian attack. By then the enthusiasm was gone. Bankrupt and broken by quarrels between disenchanted members, the company lost Virginia to the crown. As a crown colony after 1624, Virginia received the diligent and hardworking colonists of the sort we have mentioned, growing and slowly coming to a measure of prosperity.

All the while in England, in the eyes of many, conditions were rapidly deteriorating. The melancholia faintly sensed in Elizabeth's reign becomes more apparent with each year of the reigns of her Stuart successors, James I (1603-1625) and Charles I (1625-1649). In part the malaise was associated with the political failures of the Stuarts, for neither James nor Charles was able to maintain the majestic rapport of monarch and people which the Tudors had created. On the contrary, in asserting royal prerogatives, the Stuarts roused the English gentry and the Parliament which the gentry dominated. In part, too, the malaise was associated with religion. Catholicism seemed to be emerging victorious in the Europe-wide civil war between Catholics and Protestants; the Stuart kings seemed far too tolerant of Catholicism in England; and the established church of England, rather than becoming more Protestant, seemed bent on becoming more Catholic. In this situation, Puritan laymen and ministers feared for the future. "The Lord," wrote one Puritan layman, "has smited all the other [reformed] churches [of Europe] before our eyes, and has made them to drink of the bitter cup of tribulation;...I am verily persuaded, God will bring some heavy affliction upon this land, and that speedily." And religiosity, quickened by fear, evoked a greater and greater sensitivity to what were discerned as England's social ills. Thus the same Puritan layman wrote of England as "grown to that height of intemperance as no man's estate will suffice him to sail with his equal"; of trades "carried so deceitfully and unrighteously as it is almost impossible for a good upright man to...live comfortably in his profession"; of an economy groaning under the pressure of too many people "so that man the best of creatures is held more base than the earth they tread on." God, he went on, had given "the sons of men" the whole of the earth "that man may enjoy the fruits of the earth, and God may have his due glory," yet in England "people perish for want of sustenance and employment...live miserably and not to the honor of so bountiful a housekeeper as the lord of heaven and earth is." Ultimately religious and political discomfort with the Stuarts would combine and, in the 1640s, result in Civil War, the decapitation of Charles I in 1649, and the brief-lived dictatorship of Oliver Cromwell in the 1650s. But in the 1620s and 1630s England's religious and political course led some of the discomfited to think in terms of flight. Successful settlement in Virginia and the publicity attendant on it opened the possibility of flight to America.

The Chronology of Colonization

In New England, Plymouth was begun in 1620. Its origins lay in a small band of religious dissenters who, unlike the great majority of Puritans, condemned the half-way English church as utterly and completely sinful and broke both with it and their country to establish their own reformed and separate church. Having left England for Holland because they were uncomfortable as Separatists, some of them left Holland for America because they were uncomfortable as Englishmen in an alien land. They left intending to settle somewhere in Virginia under the auspices of the Virginia Company and financed by private investors. By accident or intent—and the weight of evidence points to the former—they landed in New England, growing and prospering in rural quiescence until joined to Massachusetts in 1692.

Other settlers trickled into New England in the 1620s, settling in small groups and as individuals here and there along the coast north of Plymouth. In 1628 and 1629 a major effort was begun by London merchants organized and royally chartered (in 1629) as the Massachusetts Bay Company. That same year the leadership of the company was assumed by Puritan laymen uncomfortable in the England they saw about them. In 1630, under the leadership of John Winthrop, they moved themselves, their company, their royal charter, and 700 settlers overseas to the area of Massachusetts Bay. Seven towns, including Boston, were founded the first year, more in subsequent years as the colony grew rapidly, partially because of the natural flow of Englishmen during the great migration, partially because the colony's Puritan leadership attracted other Puri-

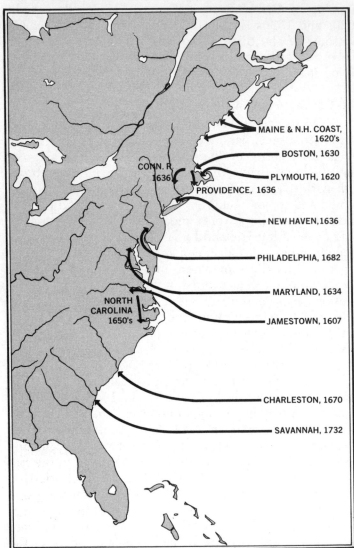

MAINE & N.H. COAST, 1620's

BOSTON, 1630

PLYMOUTH, 1620

CONN. R. 1636

PROVIDENCE, 1636

NEW HAVEN, 1636

PHILADELPHIA, 1682

MARYLAND, 1634

NORTH CAROLINA 1650's

JAMESTOWN, 1607

CHARLESTON, 1670

SAVANNAH, 1732

tans disillusioned with England. By 1635 the Bay colony boasted over 4,500 people; by 1640 almost 13,000. From Massachusetts Bay and directly from old England settlers entered what would become Connecticut. In 1635 Puritan minister Thomas Hooker led settlers from Massachusetts to found Hartford on the Connecticut River; other towns sprang up in the vicinity and in 1639 Hartford, Windsor, and Wethersfield organized a Connecticut River government separate from Massachusetts Bay. In 1637 minister John Davenport, merchant Theophilus Eaton—both Puritans—and their followers arrived from England to found New Haven on the Connecticut coast of Long Island Sound; again, other towns appeared nearby and in 1643 New Haven and the independent towns of Stamford, Guilford, and Milford joined to form a second general government in Connecticut, called the New Haven Colony. Until joined together by a royal charter establishing Connecticut in 1662, Connecticut River and New Haven continued apart.

Dissenters from the evolving religious system of Massachusetts Bay settled towns to the southward, around Narragansett Bay. Roger Williams founded Providence in 1636, William Coddington and Anne Hutchinson established Portsmouth in 1638 and Newport in 1639, Samuel Gorton founded Warwick in 1643. Ultimately the Narragansett towns were combined as one colony of Rhode Island. But as dissenters left to the south, Massachusetts Bay gradually absorbed isolated settlements to the north along the New Hampshire and Maine coast, disgorging the former only in 1680 when New Hampshire was established as a royal colony. Maine would remain a part of Massachusetts until well into the nineteenth century.

In the meantime, Maryland was established north of Virginia on Chesapeake Bay (1634) by George Calvert Lord Baltimore and his son Cecilius. Envisioned by its founders as a refuge for Roman Catholic Englishmen, Maryland soon became overwhelmingly Protestant although officially tolerant of all Christian beliefs.

During the 1640s and 1650s—England's "time of trouble," of Civil War and Oliver Cromwell—colonization was all but forgotten. But the restoration of the Stuart monarchy in 1660 was followed by a flurry of new American projects. A new "greater England" group arose, composed of courtiers, great lords of state, including the Duke of York, brother of King Charles II (1660–1685) who was to reign as James II (1685–1688). Dutch settlements on the Hudson and Delaware Rivers founded in the 1620s were granted by Charles to his brother and seized by force in 1664, becoming English New York, its Dutch population readily Anglicized. Carolina was granted to a group of royal supporters and colonial entrepreneurs (the "proprietors") in 1663. The northern part of the proprietorship already boasted settlements—Virginians who had trickled southward; Charleston, in the southern part of the grant, was settled in 1670. In 1712 the natural division between north and south was recognized in the division into the two colonies of North and South Carolina.

Profit and religion lay behind the efforts of William Penn to establish a Quaker refuge in Pennsylvania—Quakerism having emerged as a sect during the religious turmoil of mid-century England. In 1681 Penn received a royal charter to Pennsylvania and in 1682 and 1683 settlement was begun in and around Philadelphia. Delaware (settled earlier by Swedes and Dutch but part of the Duke of York's proprietary) was claimed by Penn as part of Pennsylvania under a grant from the Duke but in 1701 was established as a separate colony. New Jersey, after a complicated proprietary history, became a single government in 1702. Finally, in 1733, Georgia was founded as a bulwark against Spanish settlements in Florida and as a refuge for English debtors.

The story of the founding and development of each colony is both full and fascinating. Each had its heroic men, and its foolhardy, its times of trouble (marked by days of fast) and its good times (marked by days of thanksgiving). But there is a common history to the development of these colonies and one can approach that history by considering that they began as a scattering of Englishmen and by the 1780s had become a complex society of two and three-quarter million in the process of enunciating a national American identity. How did this happen? How did a complex society evolve from little flecks of England? What features of colonial life and society were the building blocks of a nation? In considering so broad a transformation there is danger of violating the integrity of each separate colony, an integrity clearly felt by the people themselves. "Damn my blood if I ever come into that rascally province again," a Pennsylvanian reportedly said as he crossed the border from Maryland. Even at the end of the period the American identity was merely superimposed upon an innate provincialism. And there is the danger of confusing Americanization with modernization, of forgetting that the whole of this transformation took place in a pre-industrial world where life was inevitably lived close to the soil and on a small scale, where men were typically farmers to whom the immediate society of family and village were more important than provincial, and certainly national, societies. Yet such dangers must be risked. In the sweep of American history the transformation from English to nationalistic American is the essential feature of the years through the 1780s.

Forces for Continuity and Change

Colonization along the Atlantic seaboard was the process of building not just homes and farms but societies and governments where before there was nothing. The colonists everywhere had "all things to do, as in the beginning of the world," as one wrote. Over time they built an American society. But to understand the slow process of Americanization which took place during the years from the founding of colonies through the Revolution we must first ask what the colonists *intended* to build.

The earliest years at Jamestown we can pass by. The first Virginians were too consciously transients, temporary sojourners in the New World, anxious for quick profits and a sure return to England to spend them. We must begin with people who were firmly committed to the New World, intent on staying and making their lives in America. As we have seen, such people were for the most part ambitious, acquisitive men and women who had achieved a modicum of success in England and were attracted to the New World by the lure of greater success. Their intention in America was simply to better their lot in the world and, because it would react to their own betterment, to better the New World itself. Notably this desire for improvement did not entail any desire for broad changes in the English way of life. On the contrary, the early settler immediately set about reconstructing everything he had known in England—the only change desired being that he himself be endowed with a little more of the world's goods—and always insisted that he was an Englishmen through and through.

The settlers' houses are an example. On landing in any particular colony the first settlers needed immediate shelter and set up tents, or borrowed from the Indians to build huts modeled on theirs (as in Massachusetts), or lived in caves (as in Philadelphia). But as soon as they could they built themselves houses modeled after the houses they knew in England. In essence, they attempted to transport their architecture just as they had transported their cows and pigs and seeds.

The same can be said of the settlers' institutions. What they knew in England about the law, government, defense, marriage, land tenure, agriculture, religion constituted what can be termed their "intellectual" or "cultural" baggage and this crossed the ocean with them just as did their material baggage of tools and clothes and weapons. Just as they unpacked their material baggage and began breaking the American soil with an English plow, grubbing weeds with an English hoe, clothing themselves in English woolens, and lighting their homes with English candles, so they began to erect English institutions. Their intention, in brief, was to build another England in the New World.

The effort was an impossible one. For one thing, the very nature of the settlers was a factor demanding change. They were acquisitive and individualistic. Given the necessity of reestablishing familiar institutions they unconsciously left greater room for the free play of both traits than there had been in England. The fact that the first settlements were private, profit-making ventures would have an effect on the land system and the appearance of self-government, as we shall see. The New World situation was itself a factor, for being in many respects different from the Old World, it forced changes on the settlers. We can envision, for example, a settler newly arrived in Massachusetts as he contemplated building his house. Back in the part of England from which he came houses were built with thatched roofs; consequently he built his house with thatch. But in that part of England the atmosphere was heavy with moisture. A drizzling rain, half-water, half-fog, was frequent and the thatched roofs never fully dried, hence were not fire hazards. In New England, on the other hand, there was just as much rain but it came in the form of heavy downpours. Weeks of hot, dry weather intervened between rains. The thatch dried and sparks from chimneys set it afire. One house after another burned to the ground until the settler decided that thatch would not do and turned to wooden shingles—to change!

Of course, our settler did not "invent" wooden shingles to solve his problem. Pure invention—the conceptualization of something entirely new—is a rare phenomenon in human history. Instead he borrowed the idea from his neighbor or his neighbor's neighbor, a man who, coming from a wooden shingle area of England, had built a house with wooden shingles which had not burned down.

Which brings us to still another factor for change. The colonists were a disparate lot, hence all men did not come with the same cultural baggage. One settler knew different ways and had experienced a different life in old England than a second, and the second different ways from a third. Each of the three might hold an entirely different set of values. In America there was a selection of those parts of the intellectual baggage most appropriate to the colonial situation—as in the case of wooden shingles. But there was a combination of parts, too. Thus a man trained in the law in old England, coming to a new settlement, might well value the intricacies of English jurisprudence and seek to reconstruct those intricacies in America; a clergyman, untrained in the law but devoted to and knowledgeable of the Bible, might value a Biblical concept of justice above the lawyer's concern for precise legal forms; an ambitious farmer who knew the law but slightly and felt it a hindrance to his acquisitive spirit might value and urge a simplification of the judicial structure, arguing that it should afford quick relief in cases of trespass, and little more. The fact that in the vacuum of the New World law had to be interpreted anew gave opportunity for an interaction of these disparate experiences and values and the law which emerged would consequently differ from that in England.

We must also recognize that not all elements of English culture arrived in America. The almost total absence of settlers from among the higher levels of English society would have a profound effect upon the colonial social structure, an effect we shall note in some detail. We must recognize, too, that if not all elements of English culture arrived in America, cultural elements other than English were introduced. From the very beginning the colonists were in contact with the Indian culture. By the mid-seventeenth century blacks had been injected into the colonies. In the eighteenth century, settlers from Germany, North Ireland, France and elsewhere arrived in large numbers. The evolving Anglo-American culture was inevitably affected by such contacts, both in terms of adapting particulars—the cultivation of corn adapted from the Indians, for example—and in accommodating diversity. And we must recognize that the Anglo-American colonists—always considering themselves English—were conscious borrowers from an *evolving* English and European culture. Across the Atlantic was no static society, and the Atlantic was a grand canal carrying men and ideas westward throughout the period. Hence as conditions— and with conditions, ideas—changed in England and Europe, the changes were reflected in the evolving cultural pattern in America, although more often than not the reflection was slightly distorted in the American mirror.

Finally, we must recognize that some men did have specific intentions of making changes in English ways in the colonies, and that these men had an effect upon the American pattern. Founders of colonies were, for example, frequently reformers. We have already noted in passing the quickened sensitivity to social ills on the part of Puritans during the reigns of the early Stuarts. But William Penn, the Carolina proprietors, and the founders of Georgia all shared, to some extent, the same sense of discomfort with a changing England. All looked upon individualism and ambition as detrimental to a desired sublimation of the individual to the good of society and as vitiating a desired stability in the social order. All were utopianists of a sort, thinking in terms of man's perfectibility in America.

The Puritan leaders of New England would utilize the power of the church—perfectly reformed—and of the state to bring about perfection. Men were to consider themselves "knit together" in a "bond of love"—such was the thrust of a lay sermon delivered by John Winthrop to the Massachusetts settlers of 1630:

We must love brotherly without dissimulation, we must love one another with a pure heart fervently, we must bear one another's burdens, we must not look only on our own things, but also on the things of our brethren.

The colonists were expected to settle together, and in the 1630s Massachusetts law forbade settlement beyond a half-mile from a meetinghouse. They were to honor the authority of father, magistrate, and minister, and New England law prescribed penalties for those who would not. They would deal justly with one another, and church and state would take disciplinary action against those who did not.

In Pennsylvania, William Penn anticipated not only a sanctuary for Quakerism but a "holy experiment" in Christian living. Once free of the debased and corrupted society of England, men would more easily be guided in right conduct and virtuous living by the light of God within them, the Quaker "inner light," "the precept of divine love and truth in [man's] bosom . . . the guide and keeper of his innocence." Secure on their own land, men would assume natural places in society commensurate with their property, a voice in their government equatable to their places in society, and, within a stable whole, eschew ambition, avariciousness, and quarrelsomeness.

Where Penn and the New England leaders were in a religious reform tradition, the Carolina proprietors and Georgia trustees were in a secular tradition. The Carolina founders provided for their colony a "Fundamental Constitution" by which, they hoped, a stable society could be erected and maintained by an absolute equation of power, property, and status. Thus an hereditary aristocracy would hold the largest tracts of land, wield the greatest power, and be accorded the highest status; commoners would hold small tracts, wield less power, and of course have less status; but commonalty and aristocracy would be balanced in sum, giving stability to the whole. The Georgia trustees would insure perfection by benevolent and paternal regulations, and insisted on ruling the colony from England. "The Board will always do what is right and the people should have confidence in us," they declared in 1735. They would "establish" settlers "in an orderly manner, so as to form a well regulated town"; they would tightly circumscribe the land structure by regulations meant to insure that the colony would remain a land of hard-working, diligent, and virtuous farmers. And they would forbid both rum and slavery the better to discourage degeneracy and idleness.

These attempts to effect in America reforms in the English way of the moment were all doomed to failure. They could not stand against the ambition and acquisitiveness of the settlers. "It was a very sad thing to see how little of a public spirit appeared in the country, but self-love too much," one New England leader wrote shortly after settlement. Another echoed him: "An overeager desire after the world has so seized on the spirits of many . . . as if the Lord had no farther work for his people to do, but every bird to feather his own nest." Penn, within two years of Pennsylvania's founding, would write to the colony's leading men: "For the love of God, me and the poor country be not so governmentish, so noisy and open in your dissatisfactions." The elaborate plans and regulations of the Carolina proprietors and Georgia trustees were swept away by men who sought advancement in a fluid society rather than stagnation in a stable one. Yet if such efforts to effect changes failed, they nevertheless would leave their mark, particularly in New England, for men consciously attempting one set of changes contributed unconsciously to changes from English ways of quite other sorts.

Geography, the quality of the settlers and the diversity of their cultural baggage, the absence of certain elements of English culture from the colonial's baggage, the contact with alien elements and a continuing contact with a changing Europe and England, conscious attempts to effect changes—these individually and in combination made the effort to create another England in the New World impossible. That man carries his culture around in his head, is guided in his behavior by that culture even in a removal across 3,000 miles of ocean worked to maintain a continuity between England and America. But change was inevitable—in economic thought and practice, government, basic institutions such as the land and labor systems, the structure of society, religion. Any single change might be slight, yet insignificant though each change might be, the effect of change was cumulative. The American nation, as it slowly emerged from the colonial years, would reflect both continuity and the accumulation of change.

4.

The Colonies in a Mercantile World

COLONIZATION and the transformation of Englishmen into something other than English took place in a mercantile world, hence it is with the concept of "mercantilism" that we begin to trace the pattern of continuity and change. The word itself—mercantilism—was coined by economist Adam Smith in the late eighteenth century. Most often American historians have used it merely to describe that theory of the proper relationship between the mother country and the colonies which England utilized to rationalize her various attempts to dominate colonial trade. But we will apply it to a broad system of economic regulation firmly rooted in the prevalent ideal of the sixteenth and seventeenth centuries as to man's proper relationship to his society.

Mercantilism

We have already had occasion to notice the ideal in Elizabethan England: man, fallen from Adam's state, degenerate, finding protection and comfort in society and obligating himself to subsume his degenerate urges in order that the society as a whole could prosper and perform its duty of protecting and comforting the individual. A

49

corollary of this general social ideal proceeded from the assumption that man, committing himself to the noble task of forwarding the whole society, was incapable by virtue of his degeneracy of seeing the task through. Individual men were slothful, content to take their ease while others worked, or avaricious, seeking their own gain at the expense of the whole. Hence it was incumbent upon society, through its various institutions, to protect itself and men from the degeneracy of man. Society was to encourage, cajole, even command men to contribute to the whole, all the while policing them so that they would not seek their own gain exclusively. Society used the whip, and the English poor laws of the sixteenth and seventeenth centuries were predicated upon the premise that the able-bodied pauper was criminally sinful and required punishment. More important, society turned man's degeneracy to its own advantage by appealing to his self-interest and avarice in order to bring men to contribute to the society. Bread, to use a simple example, was necessary to the society; hence society encouraged a man to bake bread by allowing him profit as an incentive, a monopoly of baking bread for the community if necessary. Yet degenerate man that he was, the baker would inevitably put self-interest ahead of society and seek a greater and greater profit. He would short-weight his customers, charge exorbitantly for his bread, use rotten but cheap flour in his baking. The society which encouraged him had also to circumscribe him by establishing fixed prices and by empowering inspectors to weigh his bread and oversee his baking.

In England, this system of thought underlay an elaborate local regulation of all phases of economic life. As political power centralized during the Tudor years, all England came to be envisioned as a single community, its parts subject to national regulation for the good of the whole. Moreover, the single community of England was envisioned as existing in a world of hostile communities— France, Spain, the north German towns, the Netherlands. A crude simile was framed: England and the others were like simple shopkeepers, buying and selling goods to each other; the one who sold more than he bought prospered, for his money bag filled with gold and silver at the expense of the others. The central authority—the crown government—naturally assumed responsibility for maintaining the well-being of the English community in the competitive situation, regulating trade beyond the boundaries of the kingdom. The customs duty, from being merely a way to raise a revenue, became a tool to encourage beneficial trades (those resulting in an inflow of bullion) and discourage those detrimental (resulting in an outward flow). Monopolies were entrusted to merchant companies. If a baker was to be given a monopoly of bread to encourage necessary baking, how much more vital to the society was the giving of a similar monopoly to encourage merchants to open a trade to Russia, the Levant, or India? Indeed, in the light of the simile, the merchant involved in foreign trade was given far more consideration and leeway in his activities than the baker, tradesman, farmer, or artisan, as well as more esteem. The merchant, it came to be said in the sixteenth century, created the wealth of England.

England's expansion and laying down of colonies introduced no new facet into this prevailing pattern of thought. As an individual was sublimated to the whole, so too were colonies. Initially the whole society to be benefited by colonization was that of England itself. But ultimately it became, in the mercantile ideal, the total complex of England and her colonies which we can term the empire, with London readily acknowledged as the source of imperial regulation. The ideal was reflected in a royal order of 1670 which charged a "Council for Foreign Plantations" to seek to regulate "by all prudential ways and means... the trade of our whole plantations [colonies], that they may be most serviceable one unto another, and as the whole unto these our kingdoms so these our kingdoms unto them."

This broad mercantile system—one defining and rationalizing a system of economic control ranging from the village baker to international trade and colonies—was not pristine in the early seventeenth century. England was in economic flux and great opportunity for individual advancement existed. Men seemed more degenerate than ever and society helpless either to curb degeneracy or turn it to society's advantage. Moreover, the philosophic basis was slowly deteriorating, to be replaced gradually by the more familiar concept of the noble individual protected in his "pursuit of happiness" by a society that was man's tool rather than man's master. In America, where ambitious men had greater opportunity to satiate their desires, the deterioration was all the more rapid. Far from sublimating himself to the community, the Anglo-American tended toward economic individualism.

In New England the early leaders, in part reacting to the deterioration of the mercantile ideal, put God firmly on the side of the ideal as part of their attempt to achieve social and religious perfection. With laws and sermons they attempted to sublimate the individual to God and the well-being of the community: Be not idle, for that is ungodly and anti-social. If you labor, labor for reasonable wages, for to take advantage of the shortage of labor in America and demand more than the labor is worth is contrary to God's word and society's good. Be not ostentatious in wearing lace, for that is sinful and, because lace must be imported, detrimental to the economy of the society. God "calls" you to your earthly profession (just as He calls you to religious duties). He requires you to be industrious in your profession so that by your industriousness you contribute to the good of the community. He rewards you with wealth for a profession well and truly pursued. But do not seek wealth for its own sake or by anti-social means. Do not sell goods for more than a "just price," for that is sinful and a crime against society. And do not hoard your wealth or squander it on frivolities, for God has given it to you only as a steward to be used for the good of the community. Laws and sermons were swept aside, how-

ever. Some men might bemoan the fact. The Reverend
Increase Mather, late in the seventeenth century, wrote
that "it was with respect to some worldly accommoda-
tions, that other plantations were erected, but *religion and
not the world* was that which our fathers came hither for."
But other men, not always without anxiety, sought their
own well-being to the exclusion of society and God.

If the philosophic basis of mercantilism deteriorated,
however, mercantilism was by no means entirely abandoned during the colonial period. Where God was put on
the side of the mercantile ideal—as in New England and
Quaker Pennsylvania—an ethic of industriousness and frugality was combined with emerging economic individualism, remaining to an extent a part of the Anglo-American
character. "Early to bed, and early to rise, makes a *man*"
—not society—"healthy, wealthy, and wise," Philadelphia's Benjamin Franklin put in the mouth of his "Poor
Richard." Here and there, too, one found stewardship carried to a logical extreme, as when the Quaker merchant
Isaac Hicks, later in the eighteenth century, quit his successful business career to devote himself to charitable
works. Nowhere did men put faith in an unfettered, completely free economy. The state was everywhere expected
to stifle greed and encourage beneficial activities. Every
colonial government retained a significant role in regulating the economy. Men were encouraged to build bridges
or maintain ferries by being given monopolies of the river-
crossings and allowed to collect tolls, subject, of course, to
governmental oversight. Government policed the market-
place with laws against forestalling and engrossing, with
inspectors of bread, beer, poultry, weights and measures,
and the like. Colonial governments, too, regulated their
harbors to the advantage of their own ships and merchants
and the disadvantage of the ships and merchants of other
colonies, even, at times, of England. Above all, however,
the colonies always existed in an economic relationship to
England defined in terms of mercantilism.

Mercantilism and the Beginnings of
Colonial Economies

Colonial theorists such as the Hakluyts defined the mercantile relationship between England and her colonies even before colonies were founded. Thinking of the outflow of bullion from England as the kingdom imported more than she exported, the Hakluyts anticipated that colonies would supply the mother country with desirable products, free her from dependence upon other European nations, and cut back the outflow of bullion. The ideas of the theorists were at variance with the realities faced by the actual colonists, however. As we noted, the theorists anticipated colonies supplying England with particular products—oranges from the Maine coast, for example— not because they knew that such products would grow in the locales to which colonists were sent but simply because such products were what England needed. More important in the long run, there was generally a gap between what the colonists and the theorists wanted. The theorists, comfortably remaining in England, could afford an abstract, national point of view. The colonists in America had a more personal point of view. Simply put, the colonists upon first landing on the American continent found their economics limited to one point: How to get enough to eat. Once they solved their initial problem they did not think, "what can I do to help the nation prosper?" but "what can I do to be prosperous myself?" Nevertheless, the colonial economies evolved within the context of the theorists' mercantilism and were affected by it.

The first settlers dispatched to Virginia and the London merchants who sent them had only the vague mercantile notions of the Hakluyts to guide them. There was talk of trading with the Indians for profitable goods which could be sent back to England, and of using the Virginia post as a point from which a search could be made for a way to the Pacific and ultimately as a transit point for rich eastern goods passing overland from sea to sea. (Geographic thought at the moment was uncertain as to the width of the continent, estimates ranging from ten or twenty miles to several hundred, with few men envisioning 3,000 miles of hills, prairies, and mountains.) Above all, however, the merchants directed the settlers to find out what valuable commodities could be grown or found in the New World and sent out specialists to experiment with wine, silk, and the like.

The colonists themselves were most interested in finding something to eat. They turned to the Indians, logically enough, and discovered Indian corn, a non-European product. In time they introduced what they could of English agricultural methods, growing English grains and raising cattle, although corn remained a major part of the diet of both men and animals. As they established themselves, they sought ways to wealth, not because the theorists demanded it but out of their own desires. They sought gold and tried what the theorists recommended. But John Rolfe's discovery of a way to cure Indian tobacco to make it more palatable to Englishmen and the subsequent importation of Caribbean tobacco seeds—better in quality than the native Virginia weed—offered them a way to wealth which the theorists had not anticipated. The settlers seized upon it, flooding England with tobacco, then the continent, for England turned early to re-exporting the crop. Indeed, the Virginians turned to tobacco to the exclusion of everything else except foodstuffs and all attempts to introduce other crops into the colony failed dismally.

To the north, the New Englanders, settling in response to social and religious impulses, were not pressured to find a proper place in a mercantile scheme. Nevertheless, they still had the task of finding, first, a means of subsistence, and second, a way to profit.

The problem of subsistence was solved as it had been in Virginia. The settlers turned to the soil to grow corn and English grains; they raised cattle both for food and to draw their plows. A way to profit was not a problem immediately, for the Massachusetts Bay area prospered

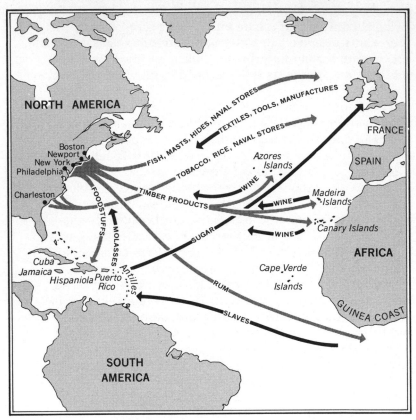

through its own tremendous growth during the early years. The first comers sold foodstuffs, seed, cattle, hewn timbers for homes, and home-manufactured implements to newcomers; the newcomers, having converted their English holdings to cash, used the cash to pay for their purchases and the old settlers paid the specie to English merchant-shippers for pots, pans, cloth—all the goods which the settlers could not produce themselves.

The cyclic economy lasted until 1640 when the great

migration (insofar as it touched New England) came to an end. Depression set in. New England found itself with a surplus of agricultural goods and a shortage of customers. The hard times eased only when Massachusetts (in the mid-1640s) began exporting its foodstuffs to the Azores, Madeira, and the coast of Spain, bartering for wine and fruits which were carried to England to pay for English goods shipped back to New England—the first of many triangle trades. In the later 1640s a second triangle was established as foodstuffs were sent to the Caribbean to be exchanged for sugar which was carried to England to be exchanged for English goods. The new trades fixed New England's economy. Overwhelmingly rural and agricultural as a section, its prosperity nevertheless depended on commerce to carry away the agricultural goods and return finished goods. The dependence on commerce gave rise to shipbuilding and trading. Boston quickly became a commercial center of the first rank, the entrepôt for all New England. The town's merchants expanded their activities beyond trade in agricultural produce, developing and controlling a domestic fishing industry and tapping the timber and fish resources of the northern coast. They entered the slave trade, establishing (in the eighteenth century) the rum-slave-sugar triangle, a relatively minor trade but one which every schoolboy memorizes. They traded in tobacco and came to dominate the colonial coastal trade. By the time of the Revolution over sixty per cent of the colonial trade—between the various colonies and from colonies overseas—was in New England's hands.

One after the other, as each of the colonies was established, they went through the same process of finding first subsistence, then profit. Subsistence always started with Indian corn, then broadened out as English agricultural methods were put into play. The finding of a source of general prosperity and profit proceeded apace. Maryland joined Virginia as a tobacco colony. New York, building on the economy laid down during its Dutch period, was devoted to fur (in the Albany area), foodstuffs (on Long Island and the lower Hudson), and commerce (in the city proper, the entrepôt for New York and northeastern New Jersey as Boston was for New England). Southeastern New Jersey and Pennsylvania were, similarly, foodstuff producing areas, surpassing New England in exports in the eighteenth century; Philadelphia, serving the area, rose as the largest city of the colonies and the second largest English-speaking city of the British empire. Moving south, South Carolina's first profitable commodities were fur and Indian slaves but by 1700 rice and by 1750 indigo assumed prominence, the latter processed into a blue dye. Georgia, after freeing itself of the unworkable utopian schemes of its founders, turned also to rice and indigo. North Carolina, producing some tobacco, was primarily devoted to the production of tar and pitch from her broad-reaching evergreen forests.

In each case the choice of the profit crop or export was made by the colonists themselves, although occasionally with an assist from England as in the case of bounties offered in the early 1700s for the production of naval stores and, later, an indigo bounty. The specific plans of the theorists—and there were many—generally came to nothing.

Nevertheless the colonists, by their own doing, fitted partially into the theoretical scheme: that they should be suppliers of desired raw materials. Tobacco was not a perfect mercantile product, for at the time Virginia turned to its production it was a minor luxury item in England. But with the addiction of England to the weed, an English source in America fitted the prescribed pattern; and with the addiction of Europe, the re-export of tobacco from England proved valuable in the balance of trade, bringing bullion into the kingdom. As early as 1640 the re-export from London of colonial products (principally tobacco) equalled in value all English exports, except textiles, combined. Similarly rice—rarely eaten in England—was sent onto the continent to England's profit. Even the foodstuff producing areas were of value, for by supplying provisions to the Caribbean islands they freed the islands to produce sugar, a favorite crop of the theorists.

The Colonies in a Commercial Empire

As colonial economies developed, as by their own doing the colonists came to fit to some extent their theoretical place as suppliers of raw materials to England, the elementary ideas of the Hakluyts were being elaborated upon in England. Exotic goods remained of prime value in the mind of English merchants and theorists; the colonists were still encouraged to produce sugar, tobacco, fur, and, of course, discouraged from sending them to France or Spain or the Netherlands. But the carriage of goods across the oceans came to be seen as having a value as well. Freightage costs, insurance, the building of trading ships, and the like were seen as mounting to a considerable sum which must not be allowed to foreigners. The notion was not entirely new; as early as the fourteenth century one finds legislation designed to protect England's shippers. The startling growth of trade, however, and the fact that in the early seventeenth century foreign ships (Dutch particularly) were as much at home in English waters as were English ships, led in the second quarter of the century to a whole series of enactments which attempted to curb so-called "interlopers." The acts were ineffective. England was involved in her "time of troubles" and the colonists were allowed to go about their own business. However, the restoration of the Stuart monarchs coincided with a high-point in that thought which envisioned England's welfare in terms of commerce, and merchants pressed for regulations which would confine the commerce of the empire to Englishmen. Two general acts of Parliament were passed in response to the pressure.

By the first of these "Acts of Trade and Navigation" (1660), certain "enumerated articles"—sugar, tobacco, cotton, indigo, ginger, and dyewoods—were to be exported from a colony only to England or another colony, a provision reflecting the classic theories of the Hakluyts. Furthermore—and reflecting the newer emphasis—no goods or commodities were to be imported into or exported from any English colony except in English-built or owned ships of which the captain and at least three-fourths of the crew were English. By the second act (1663), European goods destined for the colonies were, with few exceptions, required to be shipped from England aboard English-built and manned vessels. Subsequent acts of the seventeenth century elaborated upon these first two. When shippers began construing the act of 1660 in such a fashion as to legalize the shipment of enumerated articles from one colonial port to another and from there to a foreign port, an act was passed (1673) requiring that the shipper pay a "plantations duty" at the colonial port of clearance and post a bond which would be forfeited if the goods were ultimately unladed outside the empire. The same act authorized the appointment of customs commissioners to collect the duty and administer the bonding procedures. A general act of 1696 reiterated the earlier acts and added extensive enforcement provisions. The regular English customs service was extended to the colonies. Customs officials were authorized to obtain "writs of assistance"— judicial orders requiring all (even a guilty party) to assist the officer in opening locked doors and searching for smuggled goods. Cases arising under the trade acts were made triable in Admiralty—a jurisprudence considered so complicated that a judge alone (not a jury) was held to be competent to determine the facts—and admiralty courts were established in almost every colony.

In the eighteenth century, the Hakluyts' idea as to the colonies being a source of exotic commodities desired by the parent nation and the broader notion that the empire must profit by monopolizing its own trade continued as facets of policy. The pace of legislation slackened, however. Additional commodities were enumerated. Rice in 1704 (although the restrictions were later eased to permit the shipment of rice directly to southern Europe), naval stores in 1705, furs and copper in 1721. The flow of trade was further regulated by acts giving the East India Company the exclusive right to trade in the vast area east of Africa and west of the Americas (1698) and by requiring that all East Indian products intended for the colonies in America be first landed in England (1721). But a new mercantile notion began evolving: The colonies and mother country must comprise a completely self-sufficient unit, the colonies supplying the raw materials to be transformed by the mother country into finished goods to be sold back to the colonies. Each of the two elements—colonies and mother—would thus have a protected market and each would prosper.

Pushed by English manufacturers as they became prominent in the economy and, consequently, in politics, the new form of mercantilism was only gradually defined. Indeed, it would not fully mature until the nineteenth century when England, after losing her first empire, built a second in Africa and Asia. The immediate effect on the colonies was the beginning of legislation designed to prevent the colonies from producing finished goods in competition with the mother country. In 1696, in one of the earliest pieces of such legislation, Parliament included the colonies with foreign countries in prohibiting the sending from England of English knitting frames, an attempt to protect the English knitting industry. In 1699, the colonies were prohibited from exporting wool or wool products, even to another colony. An act of 1732 forbade the export of colonial-made felt or hats and placed restrictions on felt-making within a colony. An iron act of 1750 prohibited the erection of any new mills in the colonies for slitting, rolling, or plating iron, or of any new furnaces for making steel—at the time there were about 100 small furnaces and forges in the colonies, most in Pennsylvania, the first sign of industrialization in an otherwise agricultural-commercial economy.

In a mercantile world, the restrictions imposed on the colonies were not unreasonable. Theory on both sides of the Atlantic justified them. And the restrictions did not infringe on the natural economy of the colonies or the natural flow of trade in any significant way. There was a compatibility between England, a commercial and manufacturing center, and the American colonies, best fitted at the moment to produce raw materials from soil and forests. Moreover, commerce in the period was based upon credit, and credit upon affinities and friendships found more often within the empire than without.

There was a positive side to the mercantile scheme, too. Within the system defined by the acts, England provided an assured and stable market for colonial goods. In one of the pre-1660 acts, for example—one forbidding the export of tobacco from Virginia to any other place but England (1620)—the Virginians were given a monopoly of the English market, Spanish and Portuguese tobacco being barred, even English farmers being forbidden to have their own tobacco patches. Similarly England was an assured source of manufactured goods which the colonists, devoted to agriculture, could not produce for themselves. Southern staples sent directly to England were, in effect, paid for in manufactured goods. And while the balance of trade between the New England and Middle colonies and England was, on the surface, unfavorable to the colonies in that they shipped little directly to England in return for the manufactured items they required, the balance was made good by the free entry of the colonists into the English Caribbean islands and the resultant foodstuffs-sugar-manufactured goods triangle. Moreover English bounties subsidized the production of indigo and naval stores to such an extent that the former would end and the latter radically decline when the subsidization was withdrawn as a result of the Revolution. Even the merchants of New England, New York, and Philadelphia profited by the mercantile scheme, for while the Acts of Trade and Navigation set down the requirement that goods to and from the colonies had to be transported in English ships with English crews, "English" meant "empire," and empire included the colonists. The acts barred non-English and non-colonial ships and crews only, creating a monopoly in which colonial merchants had as much a privileged position as did English merchants.

This is not to say that there were no problems associated with the application of mercantilism on the scale of empire. There were many. No one was precluded from profiting within the system and the greater part of the colonial trade was legal, but profit could be had outside the system, too, and colonials were acquisitive men difficult to curb when their pocketbooks were concerned. And evasion was easy. Geography made absolute enforcement impossible for the coast was long, deeply embayed, sparsely populated, and the number of customs men far too few. When an opportunity for a quick profit by trading outside the system presented itself, many a colonial merchant or shipmaster turned smuggler. More often, however, the colonial, rather than violate the laws outright, found loopholes in their interpretation which, given the distance to England and the slow process of adjudication, were long in being closed. As the eighteenth century progressed, the colonial tended to count on the cooperation of customs men, their "indulgence" as it was called. Again, geography aided them. England and the elements of control were an ocean away and underpaid customs officers (more often than not half-pay deputies of absentee officers who stayed in England collecting the other half as sinecures) were free to do pretty much as they pleased. Customs men, too, were generally friends and neighbors in the relatively small colonial communities. Thus a major trade with the French and Dutch West Indian islands—New England and Middle colony foodstuffs being exchanged for foreign molasses to be distilled into rum for domestic consumption and export—was largely undisturbed by a "Molasses Act" of 1733. England imposed a prohibitive duty on the foreign products in order to protect British West Indian interests. However, as ships arrived, customs men simply peered into the holds and counted one in eight or one in ten of the casks of foreign molasses and demanded the duty on what they counted.

Exaggerated reports of evasion of the trade acts drove a wedge between colonies and mother, creating suspicion and distrust. On the one hand, the administrative provisions of the Restoration acts were badly drawn, even vague. The most conscientious colonial merchant was apt to run afoul of the acts out of misunderstanding. On the other hand, the merchant community in England was very definite as to the value of trade to England. "Trade and commerce are the pillars of prosperity and safety of England," one pamphleteer of 1673 wrote; "trade is the true and intrinsic interest of England, without which it cannot subsist." To English merchants, the trade acts were basic to the very existence of England and the slightest violation akin to treason. Making no distinction between simple misunderstanding and conscious smuggling, they saw smugglers hiding in every cove along the Atlantic seaboard. Their paranoia was communicated to those officials sent overseas to enforce the acts, men like Edward Randolph, appointed customs commissioner for New England in 1678 and surveyor general of customs for North America in 1691. Representing king and Parliament, such officials clashed from the start with colonial claims to self-regulation (claims which we will consider in detail). When, for example, colonial legislators questioned whether a given act could be applied in their colony without prejudicing the colony's political prerogatives, one such as Randolph imagined that they were questioning, even rejecting, the mercantile content of the act.

Merchants and officials came to constitute a pressure group, forever insisting that the colonials were in open defiance of England, that they were tending toward independence, and that only extreme measures would force Americans to return to their proper allegiance. The further definition of the commercial system by the acts of 1673 and 1696 was in part a result of the climate of opinion they created. In the eighteenth century, they still exhorted the government to firm up the system. In 1732, one merchant and member of Parliament went so far as to suggest that persons acquitted of trade act violations in the colonies be retried in England! But by then their influence had waned. Affairs in Europe—recurrent wars with France—were more important. And men had come to power in England in the second and third decades of the century who felt that while England might prosper more if the acts were fully enforced, she was prospering as it was and any attempt to enforce the system to the letter of the laws might be more disruptive than it was worth. What has been called the period of "salutary neglect" had set in. The suspicion of the colonies which had been engendered did not disappear completely, however.

Evasion and suspicion highlight a fundamental flaw in the mercantile scheme. As has been said, the sublimation of parts was ideally for the benefit of the whole imperial community. American foodstuffs must not be exchanged for molasses in the foreign Caribbean islands inasmuch as the trade was detrimental to the English islands and their well-being was necessary to the whole—so ran the ideal justification of the Molasses Act of 1733. But Englishmen tended to correlate the well-being of England with the well-being of the whole. Thus they failed to see the proper role New England and the Middle colonies were playing in the mercantile scheme—supplying foodstuffs to the English Caribbean. They saw only that New England and Middle-colony merchants and shippers were competing for the carrying trade with themselves and Englishmen were hostile as a result. They ignored the fact that the export of the produce of New England and Middle colony farms was necessary to the economic existence of these areas and that if empire possessions (the English Caribbean islands) were not large enough to absorb all the export, the northern areas must trade with foreign islands for whatever they could get, in this case molasses. Sugar was a more important product to England than American foodstuffs which were not even brought into England; the sale of molasses and rum to the continental colonies was vital to the prosperity of the English islands producing sugar; hence the sugar interests were to be protected and the Americans sacrified—so ran the real argument for the Molasses Act.

Colonials, too, thought in terms of their particular part of the whole, equating the well-being of their province with the well-being of the empire. Thus Virginians bemoaned the restrictions on their tobacco trade: "If this were for his Majesty's service or the good of his subjects we should not repine whatever our sufferings are for it. But on my soul it is contrary for both." A Pennsylvanian protested restrictions on manufacturing: "A vast demand is growing for British manufactures, a glorious market wholly in the power of Britain, in which foreigners cannot interfere, which will increase in short time even beyond her power of supplying . . . ; therefore Britain should not too much restrain manufactures in her colonies. A wise and good mother will not do it. To distress is to weaken, and weakening the children weakens the whole family." From their provincial standpoint the offending laws were the products of English pressure groups rather than a system of thought.

A few came to question the system of thought itself. Their society basically agricultural, their aspirations individual rather than communal, they tended to come to many of the same conclusions as the French physiocrats of the eighteenth century—economic theorists constructing a system antithetical to mercantilism. Wealth was not based on commerce, but on the products of farms and mines; each area of the globe had a way to wealth given it by nature; restrictions on trade between areas was detrimental rather than beneficial. Benjamin Franklin was to wax eloquent in his *Positions to be Examined, Concerning National Wealth* of 1768: To him commerce was "cheating," agriculture "the only *honest way* wherein man receives a real increase of the seed thrown into the ground, in a kind of continual miracle, wrought by the hand of God in his favor, as a reward for his innocent life and his virtuous industry." And to a friend he wrote:

Perhaps, in general, it would be better if government meddled no farther with trade, than to protect it, and let it take its course. Most of the statutes, or acts, edicts, arets and placarts of parliaments, princes, and states, for regulating, directing, or restraining of trade, have, we think, been either political blunders, or jobs obtained by artful men, for private advantage, under pretense of public good.

In the revolutionary and early national years such sentiments would flourish. But at the moment they were only incipient. The average man accepted regulation as part of everyday life. The merchant actively supported imperial regulations which gave him a profitable place in a monopolistic system so long as the regulations were so loosely enforced as to allow him to trade outside the system when he wanted. Certainly a New England merchant of the eighteenth century, one who thought nothing amiss in indulging, would have been the first to pound on the customs house door demanding stringent enforcement of the law if a French or Dutch ship were to sail into harbor with goods competitive with his! In the mercantilistic world, the colonial was in the enviable position of having his cake and eating it too.

5.

The Colonial Milieu

AMBITIOUS, energetic Englishmen arrived on the American coast in the early seventeenth century. Very quickly they laid down the basis of their colonial economies and established themselves within the framework of a mercantile world. All the while they were structuring the everyday institutions of life, building their farms and churches, finding their places in an evolving society. All the while, too, the process of Americanization was at work, the slow patterning of elements of continuity and change which was making of the Anglo-American a new breed of man.

The Land

In the cultural baggage of the colonists of the seventeenth century lay an elaborate, cumbersome land system, the remnant of a feudal way of life disappearing in England even as they came. Men did not technically own land, but held it under a variety of tenures which obliged them to make payments or give services, sometimes real, sometimes merely token, to a superior. Neither did they actually buy and sell land, but conveyed rights to land by almost incomprehensible legal devices.

69

In that baggage, too, lay an agricultural system based upon the village. In some parts of England, the arable land lay about the village in great open fields. Holdings were parcellated within the various fields in long, narrow strips with little or no demarcation between. The individual's lands were scattered, a strip here and there, and more often than not he worked his strips in any given field in common with his neighbors of the village. In other parts of England, however, what were called "closed" fields predominated. Here holdings were consolidated, the farmer holding two or three fields instead of many strips, cultivating the land without reference to his neighbors. The general tendency was from open to closed fields and in transitional areas both systems might exist in the same village. Surrounding the fields, whether open or closed, were common pastures and woods where the villagers grazed their livestock and from which they cut fodder and firewood.

As one might expect, English forms of tenure were brought to America. The charters from the monarchs by which colonies assumed legal existence were, in essence, conveyances of land from the king (to whom all land ultimately belonged) to the charterees. Thus Maryland was conveyed to Lord Baltimore "in free and common soccage, by fealty only for all services, and not *in capite*, nor by knight's service" (the tenure) "yielding therefore unto us," the king, "two Indian arrows of those parts" annually "and also the fifth part of all gold and silver ore, which shall happen from time to time, to be found." Charterees such as the Virginia Company, Lord Baltimore, the Carolina proprietors, and Penn conveyed land to the actual settlers in much the same way. But because theirs were commercial ventures (even to a large extent Penn's), the returns were inevitably real rather than token.

We can visualize the charterees as land salesmen. Receiving land from the crown, they had to attract settlers as customers for that land. Hence, from the days of the Virginia Company onward, charterees promised so much land to each person paying his own way to the colony plus more for each additional person, the Virginia Company in 1618 offering fifty acres per head to the individual paying the expenses incurred by that head as it crossed the ocean. A man bringing himself, his wife, and two children, for example, would be entitled to 200 acres. (That a "right" to land accrued for each "head" transported gave a name to the entitlement—"headright.") Throughout the seventeenth century the system existed in all but the New England colonies, although the details of the offer differed from colony to colony. Even in colonies under direct royal control, as was Virginia after 1624, the headright system was maintained. Toward the end of the century, however, the sale of land grants by proprietors and royal governments became common. Penn combined the headright system with cash sales in 1683, while Virginia, in 1699, began selling landrights at five shillings per fifty acres. In the eighteenth century, particularly in the royal colonies of Virginia and New York, grants of large tracts of land were made without any pretense of headright or purchase, sometimes by governors to political allies, frequently to speculators who promised to settle so many families on the land within a given period.

Regardless of such shifts in the system of land distribution, the concept of tenement—merely holding land— rather than outright ownership remained. As land salesmen (to revert to the metaphor) the charterees, in addition to attracting settlers, had to insure their own profit. Thus, while granting land on the most lenient of tenures, they insisted on the annual payment of a "quitrent." The term was, again, a feudal remnant, describing a money payment to a superior in lieu of all other goods and services which might be demanded of the holder of the land. And, again, as charterees gave way to royal government, the quitrents were retained, insuring crown governments a permanent revenue. The amount of the quitrent was nominal, one shilling per fifty acres in Virginia, four shillings per 100 acres in the Carolinas. But in sum it came to a considerable amount. The Calvert family drew approximately 4,000 pounds sterling a year from Maryland at mid-seventeenth century; the royal government in Virginia amassed a surplus out of quitrents of almost 2,000 pounds in 1691.

The tenement concept was already eroding in England. Acquisitive men were impatient with limitations on tenure and in 1656, by act of Parliament, all lands held from the king by feudal tenure were converted into freeholds. Its erosion in America was ultimately more complete, however. Where the amount of land seemed at first limitless, where all was merely wasteland awaiting the hand of man to turn into fields, the impatience was aggravated. How could crown and proprietors lay claim to all this? How could they exact a perpetual rent from those who, by their labor, gave the land a value it did not have before?

New England immediately adopted a modern alodial view of land by which ownership was absolutely vested in the individual, subject only to the paramount interest of the state. The shift was easy, for the Massachusetts Bay Company, once in the hands of the Puritan leadership, was not concerned with profits but with social perfection. Consequently it did not insist upon the tenement concept and payment of quitrents. And dominating New England as Massachusetts did, its way soon became the New England way.

Elsewhere the rhetoric of limited tenure was maintained, although every year it became more archaic even in English terms. Quitrents were too profitable to proprietors and crown governments to be surrendered. But men regularly protested proprietary rights, considered quitrents an evil imposed upon them to be evaded whenever possible, and generally tended to look upon ownership of the soil as absolute. Similarly, there was a tendency to ignore altogether the incidentals of tenement—the various "casual revenues" due to king or proprietor. It is, for example, difficult to imagine a colonial finding a whale stranded on the beach and thinking of it in terms of one of the king's or proprietors' "great fish" (as in law it really was), or of a colonial court awarding the value of a "waif's" labor to the king or proprietor. And while here and there one found conveyance of possession by ancient rite of "livery of seizin," such were exceptions. Only a few settlers took a branch from a tree and a bit of grass and pronounced, as did one, "here, son Thomas, I do before these two men give you possession of this land by turf and twig." The elaborate conveyances of England were more generally reduced to the utter simplicity of recording transfers in town or county records.

The English village came to America as well, yet it too eroded. The Virginians and Marylanders in the main seem to have come from closed field areas of old England where the village attitude was weakest, and under the headright system they received blocs of land fifty acres and larger. There was an automatic tendency to disperse along the broad rivers and bays, setting a pattern for development in the Carolinas and, in part, the Middle colonies. Local government reflected this dispersion, being organized on the basis of large counties five and ten miles in breadth and three times that in length.

In New England, however, the village was retained. Many, perhaps most, of the first settlers came from open field areas. To them the village was a strong social unit and they tended to settle in a village pattern, the village ultimately emerging as the New England town. The tendency toward the village was fostered by the strong communal feelings of the early Puritan leaders such as John Winthrop and by Puritan ministers who felt it incumbent upon all people to be within easy distance of a church. New England's way of distributing land contributed to the village physiognomy, too. Rather than granting land to an individual on the headright basis, the Massachusetts Bay Company and government generally granted the land to a group of settlers who, organizing as a town, distributed the land to the families of the group in a series of divisions or allotments, first dividing the village into houseplots and the nearest land into small farm lots, subsequently dividing the farther lands into ever larger tracts. In the first division, for example, a settler would receive houseplot and five, ten, or fifteen acres—the exact amount depending on social status, size of family, and number of cattle; he would, in addition, have rights to utilize common meadows and woods. In later divisions he would receive twenty, fifty, or hundred-acre tracts. The system begun in the Bay spread throughout the section and beyond, to western Long Island and parts of New Jersey where some New Englanders settled. It even became the basis for land speculation in New England when, at the end of the seventeenth century, colonial governments granted, sold, even auctioned town sites to investors who subsequently sold allotments to actual settlers.

Yet even in New England the close-knit village decayed. There was controversy between villagers for there were always those from closed field areas in England who objected to open fields and the village orientation. Generally the closed field men won out (as they were doing in England). There was, too, a marked movement out of the villages as families consolidated scattered holdings to form farms upon which they lived or, as the larger allotments were made, simply moved from the village to the new allotment. The common pasture and timberland was divided, "the common" being reduced to a symbolic patch of green in the middle of the village around which were situated the church and a few houses. The town remained as a unit of local government and the original village as the town seat. But for the rest, the New Englanders lived dispersed—not to the extent that the Southern and Middle colony settlers did, but to a far greater extent than historians have usually suggested.

Labor

A corollary to the land system in the colonies was the labor system, for land to be profitable required labor. On a small farm the family supplied the labor—father, mother, children, all. But when the amount of land cultivated (or which the family desired to cultivate) exceeded the capabilities of the family, or where a man of status held broad acres yet devoted his time to commerce or public service rather than the soil, extra hands were needed. Where were they to be had?

In England an agricultural system of land owners, tenants, and hired laborers was evolving. In the colonies, too, one found tenantry. The Calverts, by embellishing large grants with manorial rights, tried to institutionalize tenantry in Maryland. In New York, those receiving large grants tended to lease small tracts to tenants. Tenantry was to be found in New England, Virginia, the Carolinas, and Pennsylvania. But tenantry in an America where—relative to England and Europe—one's own land was so easily come by could never supply the amount of labor necessary. Neither could an extensive "hiring" system evolve. Few would work long for farm wages when they could have their own farms. Some system by which agricultural labor could be held to its work was necessary.

In the seventeenth century and, in the Middle colonies throughout the colonial period, the "indenture" system, an adaptation of the English apprenticeship to colonial circumstances, was the answer. By this system, those in England or, in the eighteenth century, in Germany or northern Ireland, who desired the opportunities of the New World but lacked the wherewithal to cross the ocean, contracted to work for a given number of years as servants for those who would pay their way.

The system began in Virginia where, by 1624, there were already over 400 servants in a total population of slightly more than 1,200. From there it spread to Maryland, the Middle colonies, and southward to the Carolinas. It was never, however, a significant factor in New England because of the smaller-sized farms found there.

In the first form of the indenture system, an English company involved in colonization—the Virginia Company, for example—simply sent across the ocean a number of servants under contract to work land set aside for the company, or an immigrating Englishman would merely bring along a number of servants under contract. By mid-seventeenth century, companies had faded from the scheme but the colonial was empowering an English agent to contract for him and dispatch servants to his farm or plantation. Toward the end of the century an elaborate business structure had been constructed. The would-be servant contracted with a ship-captain or one whose trade was the supplying of servants. Across the ocean, the servant's contract would be sold, often at public auction, and the labor due under it became due to the purchaser. In the eighteenth century a variation of the system—"redemption"—appeared. In this system a person, usually with his family, would pay part of the transportation cost and agree to pay the balance within a specified period of time after arrival, counting on borrowing from friends or relatives already in America, or, more often than not, contracting his own labor or that of his children to pay the debt.

Contract servitude, whether redemption or indenture, was by no means slavery. The servant was, within limits, a free man, contractually bound to his master but protected by law from abuses. His contract required that he be given adequate food, clothing, housing, and medical attention during his time of service, perhaps a freedom grant at the end—tools and clothing, occasionally a small tract of land. (Colonial governments, in an attempt to encourage servants to come, occasionally provided a freedom grant of land at public expense.) Most servants worked off their obligations in the fields, others about the house, still others as artisans, clerks, even schoolmasters. It was not unknown for a man with capital but no experience to indenture himself to a Virginian or Marylander for the sole purpose of learning the tobacco trade. Once free of service the former servant was absolutely free, and if many (as some historians argue) sank to the level of squatters and crude laborers, most undoubtedly found their way to their own land. At least a few climbed to high levels in society.

Indentured servitude in the South, however, gave way to black slavery with profound and prolonged effects.

Clearly the black man was brought to America in response to the need for labor. The first arrived in 1619 in Virginia, a few more during each succeeding decade. But the seventeenth century was basically one of white labor. Only at the end of the century did blacks begin arriving in large numbers, a result of the conjunction of three factors. The need for labor sharply increased as declining tobacco prices led planters in Virginia and Maryland to increase their acreage and as the planters of South Carolina began turning to rice and indigo. The supply of white indentured servants decreased, however, for a quickening English economy at century-end tended to keep Englishmen at home while the opening of the Middle colonies tended to absorb those Englishmen and non-Englishmen who came. Finally, the opening of the west African coast to free traders where before it had been monopolized by a Royal African Company greatly increased the number of black laborers available.

But the appearance of slavery, not an indigenous English institution, did not naturally follow from the economic factor. The need for labor could conceivably have been satisfied by the black without his enslavement.

To explain the appearance of slavery we must look at the black of the seventeenth century and at the Englishman. For his part, the black was culturally inferior when placed in the white environment. To say this is not to say by any means that the black was or is inherently inferior, only that he was a stranger to the ways of the culture into which he was brought. The black was, moreover, non-Christian in a Christian environment. And he was physically different. Culturally inferior, non-Christian, and physically different, the black was automatically set apart even from the servant society into which he came, for he was as unlike his fellow servants as he was unlike the master of the house.

That the black was different was particularly crucial, for

the Englishman of the moment had a disdain for what was different, and the disdain was seemingly proportionate to the degree of difference. Irishman, Scot, even the American Indian were objects of prejudice—although in equating the Indian with the unspoiled, virgin American continent the English mind conceived of him in paradoxical terms as "nature's nobleman" and "heathen brute" all at once. The degree of difference between Englishman and black African was altogether too great. Moreover, the type of difference—blackness—struck an ill note in a people who equated black with evil, sexuality, and the soil, and regularly placed white and black in apposition. Historian Winthrop D. Jordan, describing this apposition, quotes two lines of poetry:

> *Every white will have its black*
> *And every sweet its sour.*

then notes: "White and black connoted purity and filthiness, virginity and sin, virtue and baseness, beauty and ugliness, beneficence and evil, God and the devil." One need only read Shakespeare to sense the Englishman's feeling long before the black was introduced into the South as a laborer. Othello, for example, valiant and successful general though he was, was stigmatized as "an old black ram," "sooty," a "thing"; Desdemona's marriage to him was referred to as "her filthy bargain." Prejudice clearly preceded enslavement. One might even argue that, once the black was introduced into his society, the Englishman could evolve no other way by which the races could live together but by institutionalizing the superior-inferior relationship as master-slave.

In any event, such a relationship did evolve, and in all the colonies, for none was devoid of Africans completely although by far the greater number of blacks were to be found in the Southern colonies. The earliest blacks were legally servants but almost immediately the records hint that they were servants of a special and inferior sort. Thus, in Virginia, the white servant was considered a part of the militia and was required to train with arms; the black was barred from carrying arms. A white servant running away was punished less severely than a black running with him. The black's period of service seems to have been longer than the white's, and the phrases "servant for life" and "slave" gradually crept into the records. The black's assessed valuation in probate proceedings gradually became greater than the value of a white servant, a reflection of the longer period of labor required of him. By the late 1640s and 1650s, the peculiar status of the black servant was clearly established. In the 1650s and 1660s it was legally defined as chattel slavery. The black was not a person but property, the absolute possession of his owner, to be done with at will. He had no legal rights, but was subject to many and varied legal proscriptions.

Not all were completely happy with what had been done. Pennsylvania's Benjamin Franklin, little concerned with slavery, was nevertheless "partial to the complexion" of his own country and dismayed by the coming of the black:

While we are, as I may call it, scouring our planet, by clearing America of woods, and so making this side of our globe reflect a brighter light to the eyes of inhabitants in Mars or Venus, why should we, in the sight of superior beings, darken its people? Why increase the sons of Africa, by planting them in America, where we have so fair an opportunity, by excluding all blacks and tawnys, of increasing the lovely white.

William Byrd of Virginia disliked the effects of slavery on the whites, writing to an English friend in 1736: "I am sensible of many bad consequences of multiplying these Ethiopians amongst us" for "they blow up the pride and ruin the industry of our white people, who, seeing a rank of poor creatures below them, detest work for fear it should make them look like slaves." And a very few spoke and wrote against the institution on ethical and moral grounds: Slavery was contrary to Christianity, Quaker John

Woolman argued; liberty was "the natural right of all men equally." But once the social and economic relationship was established, once prejudice and exploitation were institutionalized—the institution constantly reinforcing prejudice and rewarding exploitation—a pattern was set which three hundred years would not completely overturn.

Land and Labor

The application of labor to land was the basis of the economy throughout the colonies. And everywhere the small farm predominated, even to the south of Pennsylvania where it is popular to imagine majestic plantation houses and thousand-acre fields dominating the scene—a picture prompted by historians who have concentrated on the total land holdings of a few rather than the pattern of land usage by the many. Even the word "plantation" was not peculiar to the South, William Logan of Pennsylvania referring to the Logan family's 500-acre "Stenton" north of Philadelphia as "my own plantation."

True, there were regional differences. To the north, in the seventeenth century, the usual farm encompassed between 50 and 150 acres worked by a family, perhaps with a few servants. To the south, the usual farm encompassed between 100 and 400 acres; the labor force, again, was the family, perhaps with a few servants or slaves. There were, too, differences equatable to the age of any particular community. As we shall see, the older the community, the smaller the size of the average holding. Some few men— the very well-to-do, particularly along the Hudson River in eighteenth century New York, in the Chesapeake Bay area, and in South Carolina—owned many thousands of acres, part under cultivation, part on speculation. But only occasionally did such large holdings form contiguous wholes. Extensive single units such as the Byrd family's "Westover" in Virginia (14,000 acres) and the Pepperrells' 1,500 acre farm in Kittery, Maine, were exceptional. The well-to-do, in general, tended to hold their land in small units, utilizing overseers or tenants. In late seventeenth century Virginia, William Fitzhugh's Stafford County holdings were considered large, but his 1,000 acres (300 of which were under cultivation) were divided into three farms or "quarters" each with its "choice crew" of laborers. In the eighteenth century the lands of Robert "King" Carter of "Corotoman," Lancaster County, Virginia, included 46 plantations in almost every part of the colony. Carter's blacks were distributed among the plantations in gangs of between 2 and 33. And in Lancaster County at mid-century 212 of 245 landowners owned less than 400 acres; 167 of the 245 owned slaves, 134 owning between 1 and 5, 30 between 6 and 20, the largest number on any single farm being 33.

The land pattern with its small units was in part dictated by the type of settler who arrived. Everywhere he sought land but more often than not had little wherewithal to obtain it. Cheap as land was, the average man could afford just so much and was content with what his town awarded him in New England, what was due him by headright, or what he could purchase. The result was a fragmentation from the very beginning. If a man rose in wealth and sought to purchase more cultivated land, he purchased from others less successful (who more often than not sought land elsewhere) to gain not a large contiguous parcel but several small units. If two large landholdings were merged by marriage, as was frequently the case, the result was not one large plantation but a scattering of small units. And if, in the eighteenth century, a man of means obtained by grant a large bloc of wilderness land on speculation, men of smaller means were his most numerous customers, hence he sold in small units, expanding the fragmentation into new areas.

In part, too, the size of agricultural units was dictated by economy of operation. Given the tools of the time, the cultivation of grain imposed an upper limit on the amount of land on any working unit; and grain was not only the major product of the North, both for consumption as well as export, but a major subsistence crop in the South, where only a portion of the land was given over to staples. Moreover, tobacco in the Chesapeake area was not (as cotton would be in the nineteenth century Deep South) a crop which could withstand careless tending. Tobacco culture involved a series of painstaking operations, from the planting of infinitesimal seeds in seedbeds, through transplanting to the fields, worming, weeding, removing suckers and bad leaves, to cutting, curing, and packing. A larger force than 20 to 30 blacks on a single farm larger than 400 acres would have made impossible the careful oversight that tobacco required. Similarly, in South Carolina, a rice or indigo plantation of more than roughly 300 acres would have led to inefficiency and waste.

If there was a basic similarity in the pattern of land usage, there was a basic and highly significant dissimilarity in the internal trade pattern. The application of labor to land in the Northern colonies produced foodstuffs and, as we have seen, the necessity of exporting farm produce gave rise to commerce and the great entrepôts of Boston, New York, and Philadelphia. Commerce and urban growth opened avenues to wealth apart from the land, for men with a bit of capital to invest could rise rapidly by speculating in city lots, milling, shipbuilding, mercantile activities, services such as printing, to an extent manufacturing.

To the south, land and labor produced staple crops for export. But with its broad, navigable rivers, the Chesapeake area had no need of a commercial entrepôt. In the seventeenth century ships merely entered the rivers to buy and sell at the planters' docks, the larger planters serving as merchants for the smaller, collecting their neighbors' tobacco for sale to the ships and buying goods wholesale for retail to the same neighbors. The trading pattern was dispersed and the planter was, in a sense, his own merchant. No real way to wealth except through the land developed. In the eighteenth century the pattern shifted. Men settled inland, beyond the reach of ocean-going ships; English and particularly Scottish merchant houses established factors in the tobacco colonies to buy and sell goods on consignment and credit. Where the factors settled, small villages appeared—Norfolk, Yorktown, Richmond, Alexandria, Baltimore. The simplicity of a staple trade was such, however, that elaborate facilities and services were unnecessary in any but Baltimore which ultimately tapped the rich grain trade of Pennsylvania's Susquehanna River Valley. Except for Baltimore the new villages, together with southern colonial capitals such as Williamsburg and Annapolis, grew to but small towns, nothing more, and even Baltimore was tiny compared to the great ports of the north. The road to wealth in the Chesapeake was, consequently, still limited to the land. And the upper levels of Chesapeake society came to consider the limitation something of a virtue. A landed ethos developed: They were in the tradition of the English landed gentry, theirs the only proper way to wealth, trade (particularly as theirs seemed dominated by detestable Scotsmen) and other such occupations were demeaning. The ethos connected with the land rather than the land pattern itself came to set the Chesapeake apart.

Farther south, Charleston combined the attitudes of the northern areas and the Chesapeake to form a unique pattern. Settlement had tended to be centralized from the beginning (when the colony exported no more than furs and Indian slaves); the prominent Carolinian held land around the town, farming it with servants, all the while trading in Charleston. The turn to rice and indigo did not break the pattern. The way to wealth for a Carolinian was still a combination of agriculture and commerce, and the successful Carolinian came to display a landed ethos and attitude of gentility which surpassed even Chesapeake society, together with an ardor for business which would not have been out of place in Boston. The former masked the latter, however—it was almost as if the Carolinian was so ardently genteel because he was so adept at business and a little ashamed of it—and Charleston had a gaiety and sophistication unsurpassed in the colonial world.

An Expanding America

This New World of farms and commerce was marked by steady growth. During the great migration of the early part of the seventeenth century Englishmen arrived by the thousands. The pace slackened in the 1640s, revived briefly in the 1660s, and slackened again. But the population continued to grow as a result of a natural increase, almost doubling every twenty-five years. And the growth of population augmented mobility among the colonials. A New England town or a Virginia county, settled early in the seventeenth century, its economy based upon agriculture and its people oriented to the land, was relatively quickly filled, even overcrowded. Fathers with two or three sons found it difficult to establish those sons upon land of their own within the community; the sons found it even more difficult to find land for the grandsons. Sons and grandsons, when they did receive land, received far less than had their fathers and grandfathers. In dramatic fashion, historians of New England towns have shown this phenomenon. In Dedham, Massachusetts, the fathers received an average of 210 acres during their lifetimes; in Watertown, 126 acres; in Medfield and Sudbury, 150 acres. Their grandsons of the eighteenth century had available but an average of 38 acres apiece in Dedham, 17 acres in Watertown, 44 acres in Medfield, 56 acres in Sudbury. As a consequence of such overcrowding, the sons and grandsons, in increasing numbers as time went on, left the older communities to find land and economic independence in newly settled communities.

In the seventeenth century the thrust outward from the

AN EXPANDING AMERICA
Distribution of population between 1650 and 1790

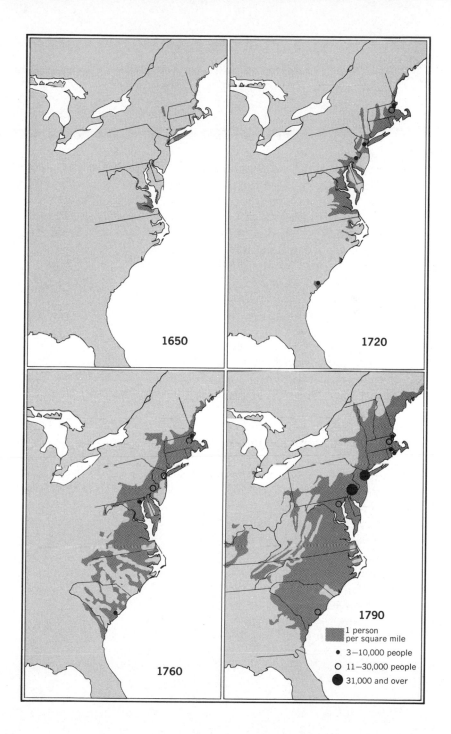

1650

1720

1760

1790

1 person
per square mile

• 3—10,000 people

○ 11—30,000 people

● 31,000 and over

older settlements was to the north and south from the points of initial entry onto the continent. Thus the Virginians expanded north from the James River to the York, Rappahannock, and Potomac, and southward to Albemarle Sound in North Carolina. Maryland expanded northward from the first settlement at St. Mary's near the Potomac and across the Chesapeake to the "Eastern Shore." New Englanders pressed north and south from the area around Boston harbor and into the interior along the broad Connecticut River. The rate of exodus and resettlement kept pace with the population as it doubled and redoubled and in the eighteenth century the colonists thrust westward, to and into the White, Green, and Berkshire mountains of New England, across the southern Piedmont, into and finally beyond the Appalachian Mountains.

If the pressure of a natural population increase forced mobility upon the initial English population and brought about geographic expansion, such was only part of the story. For toward the end of the seventeenth century immigration into the colonies quickened as non-English immigrants began arriving in significant numbers. William Penn actively solicited settlers for his Pennsylvania from among German Quakers and Pietists, and accepted a band of Welshmen who desired to "live together as a civil society to endeavor to decide all controversies and debates amongst ourselves in a gospel order"—a desire which Penn could not but approve. French Protestants (or Huguenots) began arriving after the revocation in 1685 of the Edict of Nantes which had insured them a privileged position in France; by 1700 some 4,000 were scattered through New England, another 1,000 in New York, 4,000 more in South Carolina.

In the eighteenth century the number of non-English arrivals grew to phenomenal proportions. Germans came, fleeing the depredations of war along the Rhine, religious persecution, the exactions of petty princes, and the remorseless pressure of economic change—a combination of ills aptly described in the opening chapters of Voltaire's

Candide. By 1727 they were arriving at the rate of 2,000 a year, while in the four years following 1750, 25,000 stepped ashore. For the most part they came to Pennsylvania. Some were affiliated with religious groups and tended to settle as communities on the outer fringes of English settlement—Mennonites, Amish, Dunkards, River Brethren, Schwenkfelders, Moravians. The rest came singly or with their families, utilizing the redemption system to pay their passage. But they too eventually settled on the fringe of the English, contributing to the creation of a German pale which extended in a great arc about Philadelphia from Easton on the Delaware to the Maryland border and from the western environs of Philadelphia to the Susquehanna and beyond.

Scotch-Irish came, too. Scots who had settled in northern Ireland early in the seventeenth century, the Scotch-Irish (or Ulster Scots) were subjected to rack-renting by absentee landlords and struck by periodic crop failures. In five great waves, the first in 1717–1718 and the last in 1771–1775, they left Ulster for America, some settling in New England but most landing in Philadelphia. As did the Germans, the Scotch-Irish tended to move to the outer fringes of settlement after completing in the English area whatever period of service was required to pay passage money.

All told, perhaps a quarter million Scotch-Irish arrived and 100,000 Germans. The two groups came to predominate in the Pennsylvania backcountry and from there flowed southward through the great valley system of the eastern Appalachians to settle western Maryland and the Shenandoah Valley of Virginia. Passing the mountain gaps in southern Virginia, they pressed southeastward onto the Carolina Piedmont and southwestward to the headwaters of the Tennessee River. There were other nationalities represented among the non-English—for example, highland Scots settled along the Cape Fear River in North Carolina and Irish and Swiss along the Mohawk in New York—but none were as significant as these.

The non-English brought their own language and customs to the New World. But colonial America was not a pot in which diverse cultures were melted down and amalgamated to form something new. To the contrary, eighteenth century America is more aptly compared to a mosaic than to a melting pot (although this in itself was a difference from England). The overall cast of the mosaic—the dominant element of the design, so to speak—was always English. It could hardly be otherwise, for those of English origin arrived first, established the basic institutions and values of the society, and always predominated numerically and in terms of wealth and power. But the minor elements of the design, lending complexity and interest to the whole, were the various national groups. Each such group, with significant exceptions such as the Huguenots who were quickly absorbed into the English culture, held itself apart from the English and from each other, the lines between sharp and crisp. Thus in Pennsylvania Gettysburg was a German town, nearby Carlisle Scotch-Irish, each tolerant of the other but no more. Only time would break down this mosaic (while creating others), although even today the Pennsylvania German (or "Dutch," being a corruption of "Deutsch") countryside is easily recognizable by the observant traveler along the Pennsylvania Turnpike.

The English community, for its part, looked askance at the hordes of non-English. The Scotch-Irish were rabble, the Germans "Palatine boors." "Why," asked Franklin,

should the Palatine boors be suffered to swarm into our settlements, and, by herding together, establish their language and manners, to the exclusion of ours? Why should Pennsylvania, founded by the English, become a colony of aliens, who will shortly be so numerous as to Germanize us instead of our Anglifying them, and will never adopt our language or customs any more than they can acquire our complexion?

The attitude was not consistent, however. The distrust of the foreigner was matched by the time-honored image of

America as a land of promise—an image of another "Eden" dating back to Columbus—and the realization that in a new world every pair of hands was an asset. Franklin again: America was a place

> *Where the sick stranger joys to find a home,*
> *Where casual ill, maim'd labor freely come.*

Nativism and the idea of a society open to all comers would commingle in the American mind for long.

The sheer increase in numbers of people is, in terms of the period, the most significant factor of the immigration, far more significant than the introduction of cultural diversity. From less than 300 in 1607 (on the Sagadahoc and at Jamestown), the colonial population grew to just over 200,-000 by the end of the seventeenth century and increased tenfold (to approximately 2,000,000) by 1763. New people and new lands meant an ever-greater production of agricultural goods, greater consumption, an augmented need for services, increased commerce. The economy was, in the economist's words, an expanding one with the rate of expansion (and the resultant prosperity) significantly greater in the eighteenth than in the seventeenth century. Indeed, the splendor of the eighteenth century—seen so clearly in its magnificent architecture and the elaborate, urbane culture of its cities—is directly attributable to the expanding economy.

Social Restructuring

Englishmen arriving in America in the early seventeenth century brought with them a notion of society as ordered and hierarchic, holding that there were (very properly) higher and lower degrees among men and that individual men should have wealth, political power, and social status commensurate with their degree. God himself, they believed, had established that men should stand in proper social orders, ordaining that "in all times some must be rich, some poor, some high and eminent in power

and dignity, others mean and in subjection." English society—and the first settlers knew no other—had been so
ordered. For in England there were those who properly
counted in society, the small minority of titled nobility
and, a step down, the untitled gentlemen, who governed
England under the king; there were those who properly
counted for little, "the middling sort" of farmers and
tradesmen; and there were those who properly counted
for nothing, the common laborers and servants, the paupers and vagrants. There was fluidity of a sort in England,
more so than in the rest of Europe, and a man might pass
from degree to degree. Nevertheless the lines between
degrees were rigidly observed. As G. R. Elton, an English
historian, has written, "a nobleman exacted higher respect
and obedience than a gentleman, a knight more than an
esquire," and all of "gentle" birth and breeding more than
a shopkeeper, tradesman, artisan, yeoman farmer, or hired
laborer. The criteria of more than common rank were a
subtle compound of title, family, acquaintances, wealth,
influence, manners, dress, and land.

If such notions of the proper ordering of society arrived
in America, however, a fully ordered English society did
not arrive. The settlers were almost all of the "middling
sort." There were practically no noblemen, no men of title
among them, and one can count the exceptions on one's
fingers; there were, therefore, very few to assume automatically the highest places in society and bring to
America the experiences and values of the highest levels
of English society. Neither were there the very lowest
elements of English society in any significant numbers.
The settlers had, therefore, to recreate an ordered, hierarchic society ranging from men of high to men of low
degrees out of a single English "middling" degree.

In the process of restructuring a society the time-honored English distinctions, the attributes which separated
gentle from lowborn, simply disappeared. No one, to all
intents and purposes, was titled or had "family" among
the first colonists; few had the aura of gentleman which

manners and dress created; and inasmuch as most of the settlers very quickly had land, the possession or lack of land could not serve to distinguish between ranks. Only one thing truly separated one settler from another: Some arrived with more capital than others, capital in any one of a number of forms—money itself, or credit, or acquaintances and relatives in the colony who had already achieved a modicum of success and could introduce the newcomer to the sources of money and credit, or ability and perseverance, or even mere luck. And in the expanding colonial economy the man with such capital could rise easily above his fellows.

In this situation the settlers—all of a piece in terms of degree—came to be sorted out into diverse degrees on the basis not of what they were but of what they had, being accorded social and political position on the basis of the economic position they had won for themselves. Wealth became the criterion of status, wealth in the form of commercial interests, ships, and land in the coastal areas of the North and again in South Carolina, or of land alone in the Chesapeake area and in the interior everywhere. There was no standard figure which a man's estate had to reach in order for him to be accounted of "the better sort." The whole question of status was relative. A man amassing an estate of 100 pounds sterling was a gentleman, a social leader, and a political leader in a community in which the average estate was but ten pounds, while in another community, where gentlemen had 1,000 pounds, he might count for little.

The emergence of all ranks from one, and of wealth as the criterion of status, introduced a fluidity into colonial society far greater than that of England. Because only wealth was a criterion and the new land had so many opportunities for wealth, men rose (and fell) in position faster. Thus William Pepperrell, in 1670, arrived in Maine from Devonshire, England, via the Newfoundland fisheries, invested small shares in fishing voyages, became a principal owner of a vessel or two, and went on to found one of the major commercial fortunes of the northeast. At about the same time, William Byrd, son of a London goldsmith, arrived in Virginia. Inheriting lands from an uncle and marrying into the family of an older landed settler, he laid the foundation of one of Virginia's great fortunes and himself rose to membership on the governor's council.

The fluidity was more marked in the early years of any particular community, for in the beginning of settlement the process of creating a hierarchic structure out of the single degree was in process while as time passed, as communities became relatively crowded, an upper class came to exist as something of a self-perpetuating group, the founders of families passing their gains to their sons who thus had a greater store of capital to start life with than the average. The process has been traced for one Pennsylvania county. In 1693, shortly after settlement, wealth in the county was remarkably evenly distributed, the wealthiest ten per cent of the population holding less than one quarter of the taxable wealth of the community; a hundred years later, however, the wealthiest ten per cent held a third of the county's taxable wealth. In terms of the whole of the Anglo-American shore, the distinction can be generalized as one between the seventeenth and the eighteenth centuries, fluidity being more marked in the earlier than in the later century by which time prominent families had assumed colony-wide status: Wentworths in New Hampshire; Olivers, Hutchinsons, Otises in Massachusetts; Trumbulls and Winthrops in Connecticut; De Lancys and Livingstons in New York; Carrolls and Dulanys in Maryland; Byrds, Randolphs, Lees, Carters in Virginia; Pinckneys and Leighs in South Carolina.

As time went on men came to proclaim their status by a conspicuous show of the wealth they were accumulating in an expanding economy—for example, the lavish, grandiose houses of the eighteenth century. And the colonial *parvenus* quite consciously came to emulate the English upper classes, adopting what they assumed to be the manners, dress, education, and pride of family of the English

gentlemen to create distinctions additional to wealth between themselves as the better sort and a generality
vaguely divided between the middling sort of farmers,
shopkeepers, and artisans and the inferior sort of laborers,
common tenants, seamen, servants serving their inden-
tures, and transported convicts. (Slaves were not even considered, while professional men—doctors, lawyers,
ministers, schoolteachers, who were not of the better sort
by virtue of independent wealth—were consigned to that
awkward position reserved for them in most societies: social half-breeds admitted as equals by those who knew
themselves superior.) Among the better sort, handbooks
taught the "art" of proper behavior—Richard Allestree's
A Gentleman's Calling and Henry Peacham's *The Com-
pleate Gentleman*, wherein one learned that fortitude,
prudence, temperance, justice, liberality, and courtesy
were cardinal virtues for the gentleman. The appurte-
nances of a successful, wealthy, and ever-more idle group
appeared—the arts and letters, music, private libraries.
"Any young gentleman," wrote one observer, "is pre-
sumed to be acquainted with dancing, boxing, playing the
fiddle, and small sword, and cards." The tendency was
most marked in coastal Virginia, Maryland, and South
Carolina where large landholdings set off the few on a
basis most compatible with English notions of social grada-
tions, and where slavery buttressed the position of the
large landowners. It was less marked to the northward
where landholdings were not as important and fortunes
were more closely tied to commerce, the less gentlemanly
way to wealth. North and South, however, it was all a
crude rendition of the English and European original, a
travesty, as one European gentleman touring the colonies
observed, the exaggerated poses of "aggrandized upstarts"
who "never had an opportunity to see, or if they had, the
capacity to observe the different ranks of men in polite
nations or to know what it is that really constitutes that
difference of degrees."

If society was becoming less fluid in the older communi-

CONTRASTING SIDES OF COLONIAL LIFE

A New England Farmstead

Casking Tobacco In Virginia

LOADING HAY IN NEW ENGLAND
From an early twentieth-century photograph

A COMMERCIAL WHARF

ties and in the eighteenth century in general, a complete hardening of society never set in. True, wealth continued to accumulate in the hands of fewer and fewer families; Anglo-American society increasingly polarized between those who had much and those who had little. But the tradition of fluidity was too firmly established. It was perfectly obvious that one's "betters"—that is, those wealthier—were inherently no better than oneself, that a Byrd or Pepperrell (or the father of the current Byrd or Pepperrell) had started life on the same plane as a Smith or Jones, while a Smith or Jones, or a son, could conceivably rise to the heights of a Byrd or Pepperrell. Reality bore Smith or Jones out. Men still rose in position in the long-settled areas, successfully competing with entrenched families, even if far less frequently; and there were always new areas being settled, particularly to the west, where the process of sorting men into degrees from the single middling degree that dominated all new settlements was still in progress. Given the tradition and continuing fact of social mobility, there was less inclination to pay one's betters the outward forms of respect, the scraping and bowing of Europe. One was deferential. The hierarchic organization of society remained a natural ordering of men to be honored, and besides, a man who dressed and talked like a gentleman was undoubtedly a man of at least some wealth, and wealthy men were powerful men. But there was a basically free attitude toward the gentleman, and toward those things which the English and European gentleman considered the gentleman's exclusive province, an attitude occasionally annoying to the visiting European gentlemen who were used to respect. A French traveler noted in 1772 that:

... the poorest laborer on the shore of the Delaware thinks himself entitled to deliver his sentiments in matters of religion or politics with as much freedom as the gentleman or scholar. Indeed, there is less distinction among the citizens of Philadelphia, than among those of any civilized city in the world. Riches give none.

For every man expects one day or another to be upon a footing with his wealthiest neighbor.

And there was rapport downward on the part of the better sort:

The laborious part of men, who are commonly ranked in the middling or lower class, are accounted the strength and honor of the colony, and the encouragement they receive from gentlemen in the highest stations is the spring of industry, next to their private advantage. . . . Hence we see gentlemen when they are not actually engaged in the public service, on their farms, setting a laborious example to their domestics, and on the other hand we see laborers at the tables and in the parlors of their betters enjoying the advantage and honor of their society and conversation.

God and Man

We have approached the colonial milieu in a secular fashion, dealing with land and labor, economics and social structure, and leaving aside the sacred aspect of life. Yet certainly in the seventeenth century the sacred everywhere gave dimension and meaning to life. God—sometimes merciful, often wrathful, always awesome—was sovereign over the earth and over men. He was the creator and man, from the time of Adam's fall, a favored but imperfect creation. He it was who bestowed fortune or misfortune in this world, salvation or damnation in the next, who determined the natural and supernatural order of things for His own purposes, and whose will as partially revealed in the Bible was man's best explanation of and guide through life. In the shadow of this awesome deity, religiosity was pervasive. Men defined themselves and the world about them in godly terms, and looked to churches and ministers as central to the everyday life of their communities.

The pervasiveness of religiosity, however, was matched by the pervasiveness of controversy as to the proper nature of formal religious expression and institutions. The

England from which the first settlers came was divided on religious issues as Puritans of various degrees and kinds opposed in different ways the creeds and practices established by law. So too were the settlers divided. Thus in 1609 word came to England that among the Virginians there was "unhappy dissension" in Jamestown, that many rejected the teachings of the minister in the colony, refusing "to go to his service and hear his sermons, though by the other part he was supported and favored." Tiny Plymouth was involved in religious disputes, expelling the Reverend John Lyford in 1625. The leadership of Massachusetts Bay was intent on establishing God's perfect church as part of their perfect society, but even there arguments broke out as individual Puritan ministers differed as to their interpretation of God's will. Roger Williams, in clashing with his ministerial colleagues—among other things he argued that the civil government could not rightfully intervene in religious matters, even to the extent of simply enforcing Sabbath observance—was only the most vehement and stubborn of many controversialists. Moreover, the ardent preaching of the Massachusetts ministers provoked among laymen an enthusiastic personal religiosity, the most spectacular episode being that of the mid-1630s when Mistress Anne Hutchinson, prompted by the preaching of the Reverend John Cotton, swept Boston into religious anarchy.

In time a semblance of order was imposed on the religious scene in Virginia and New England. The Virginians legally instituted the established Anglican church of England. The New England ministers—at least those of Massachusetts Bay, the Connecticut River and New Haven towns, and Plymouth—gradually formalized a New England or Congregational "Way," abetted in their efforts by civil authorities anxious for order, tranquility, and unity. The ministers purified the ceremonies of the English church and limited membership to those of high morals, good conduct, and right belief (as against the English church which theoretically embraced all members of the

community). Denying the validity of the hierarchic structure of the English church, they lodged all ecclesiastical
authority in the individual congregations, although assuming for themselves as God's messengers a position of
primacy and erecting a vague, intercongregational structure of ministerial meetings, councils, and synods by
which the ministry could police itself and insure the
preaching of "right" doctrine.

It was, however, only the semblance of order, not the
reality. Anglican and Congregational orthodoxies were
façades behind which men and women in their individual
towns (in New England) and parishes (in Virginia) prac-
tised individual religions more attuned to their own community life than to any orthodox position. In Virginia, the
law proclaimed Anglicanism but there were no archbishops, bishops, and archdeacons, no ecclesiastical courts,
nothing of the hierarchy of the English church to maintain
a single discipline and doctrine in every parish in the
colony. There was only a scattering of isolated ministers
and the lay vestries of the local parishes which controlled
the churches, even to the extent of hiring and firing their
ministers at will. Decentralized and lay-controlled, the
Virginia churches were a mosaic of practices and beliefs.
In one parish, a Presbyterian-type ministered happily to
an ostensibly Anglican church; in another, a man of almost
Baptist leanings served on an Anglican vestry; in a third,
an Anglican vestry applied to New England for a Congre-
gational-type minister when no other minister was available for hire locally. And everywhere there were "small
alterations" in ostensibly Anglican services for, as one minister wrote, it was "impossible for a clergyman to perform
[his] duty according to the literal direction of the [Angli-
can] rubric; for were he too rigorous in these respects, by
disobliging and quarreling with his parish, he would do
more mischief in religion, than all his fine preaching and
exemplary life could retrieve."

In New England, ministers still disputed with one another, although for appearances' sake they agreed to disa-

gree only in private—an agreement which broke down during the second half of the seventeenth century when the ministers aired their differences in vehement diatribes. More to the point, ministers and their congregations argued, and for the most part ministers either lost their pastoral positions by virtue of their stubbornness or accommodated their views to the views of their congregations. As in Virginia, a welter of confused practices and beliefs hid behind the façade of orthodoxy.

And finally, outside of Virginia and New England, there never was, in the seventeenth century, even the semblance of order, only an array of beliefs and disbeliefs, compounded by the fact that in many areas (Rhode Island, Protestant areas of Maryland, and North Carolina, for example) there were few or no ministers and religion was completely a matter of individual and community decision. One observer, for example, commenting on a lay religious gathering in North Carolina, wrote of "a strange mixture of men of various opinions but most Anythingarians." Quakerism, entering the colonies around mid-century, spread swiftly in such areas, for denying the efficacy of ministers and preaching dependence on an "inner light," the Quaker messengers offered a solution to the religious needs of people bereft of ministers.

Order emerged from chaos in direct relationship to events in England. There the effort, early in the seventeenth century, to enforce a single Anglican persuasion in the face of disparate beliefs had contributed to the coming of civil war. In the aftermath of war and Cromwellian commonwealth, the state gradually abandoned all efforts to enforce compliance to a single Anglican religious system and effected toleration of dissent from established ways. The Church of England (Anglican) remained a state church, the monarch its titular head, but other religious systems were free to evolve. In this situation an Anglican persuasion, together with its competitors—Presbyterian, Baptist, Quaker and the like—assumed a self-conscious corporate identity. *The* church, from being the religious facet of an entire society, became a number of separate denominations within the society, and each denomination sought to expand overseas.

Toward the end of the seventeenth century and early in the eighteenth Anglican ministers, imbued with this corporate sense, appeared in the colonies in unprecedented numbers, spurred on by Henry Compton who, as Bishop of London, had a claim to the religious oversight of the colonies. The newly arrived ministers were aghast at the colonial confusion, and they interpreted what they saw as irreligion. Quite consciously they set about effecting reforms which would bring the Anglican churches in the colonies, particularly those of Virginia, in line with the English, while to the north they began warring upon Congregationalism.

The Anglican ministers and missionaries were partially successful. Anglican churches made their appearance in New England despite the opposition of New England's governments and ministers. (England's toleration was extended to the colonies by royal edict, forcing New England to accept what it did not want.) Formal Anglicanism spread rapidly through the South, Maryland and the Carolinas at the turn of the century joining Virginia in establishing Anglicanism by law, legislating parish lines and authorizing vestries to assess the inhabitants for the maintenance of the churches and support of the ministers. But laymen had controlled religion too long and the Anglican ministers found that they had to be content to be but employees of the churches rather than governors, their influence dependent upon their personalities and the acceptability of their preaching. Nevertheless, the ministers were strong enough to effect a cleansing of the most disparate elements within the churches, and these disparate elements came together in their own dissenting churches. (The toleration decreed from England which helped Anglicanism in New England helped dissenters elsewhere.) Aided by their English brethren, the dissenters organized Presbyterian synods, Baptist conventions, and Quaker yearly meetings. Quaker settlement in New Jersey and Pennsylvania, the spread of Anglicanism throughout the Middle colonies, and the coming of the non-English with their own churches—the various sects, the broader Lutheran and German Reformed, the Presbyterianism of the Scotch-Irish—contributed to the denominational trend. And Anglican, Baptist, all forgot the universal church of Christians as, solicitous of denominational purity, they stressed in tracts and sermons the particulars which set them apart from each other.

All the while the churches were abandoning their broad social role. The New Englanders, in reforming their churches, divested them of certain legal functions which had fallen within the province of clerics in England—marriage, for example, and the probate of wills. Similarly, while the secular authorities in New England supported the churches and made of the Congregational the established church of the area, laymen and clerics alike consciously separated the functions of the church from those of the state. Can an individual "be a civil magistrate and a ruling elder [of the church] at the same time," the Boston Church asked in 1632. No! "The government of the church is as the Kingdom of Christ is, not of this world, but spiritual and heavenly. . . . The power of the keys is far distant from the power of the sword." Unlike England where the established church was involved in the political processes to the extent of its bishops sitting in the House of Lords, the colonial minister had no special political privilege. Each church and denomination played a social role in relationship to its own members, but only the state encompassed everybody, hence of necessity it came to assume the broad responsibilities which atomized religion was laying down.

The churches were losing their hold on men. The phenomenon was not unique to America. Everywhere in the West, it would seem, a concern for this world, its profits and its pleasures, was superseding a concern for the next. The churches remained. God had to be served; certain fundamental but *pro forma* ordinances had to be obeyed —to all but Quakers one's children had to be baptized, for example. And in the church on Sabbath, one paid one's respects to the Creator, received the necessary sacraments, heard God's word read and His servant speak—too often obtusely. But it was in the field or counting-house that life was truly lived.

Among the educated there was an exaltation of reason to the denigration of revelation. Mechanical laws governing the universe had been discovered, and Sir Isaac Newton's postulates were replacing heavenly caprice in the consideration of natural phenomena. The Enlightenment was abroad in Europe and England, and America was not unaffected. The weight of an awesome Jehovah was being lifted from men. A moderate Deism spread—a logical demonstration of the existence of God, the appropriateness of morality, and the irrelevance of formal religion. Franklin epitomized it when he wrote to his father in 1738: "The Scriptures assure me, that at the last day we shall not be examined what we *thought*, but what we *did;* and our recommendation will not be, that we said, *Lord! Lord!* but that we did good to our fellow creatures." And again in later life he was to write:

I believe in one God, creator of the Universe. That he governs it by his Providence. That he ought to be worshipped. That the most acceptable service we render him is doing good to his other children. That the soul of Man is immortal and will be treated with justice in another life respecting its conduct in this. These I take to be the fundamental principles of all sound religion, and I regard them as you do in whatever sect I meet with them. As to Jesus of Nazareth . . . I think the system of morals and his religion, as he left them to us, the best the world ever saw or is likely to see; but I apprehend it has received various corrupting changes, and I have, with most of the present dissenters in England, some doubts as to his divinity.

Here and there a clergyman echoed the same sentiments. Thus Jonathan Mayhew of the West Church, Boston, preluding Unitarianism, preached not of a God who damned all mankind for Adam's sin, then saved a few by His own dispensation, but of God the kindly sovereign governing "his universal kingdom, according to those general rules and maxims which are in themselves most wise and good."

Piety, or the love of God is the first and principle thing in religion. ... The love of our neighbor ... necessarily flows from the love of God. ... It is practical religion, the love of God, and a life of righteousness and charity, proceeding from faith in Christ and the gospel, that denominates us good men and good Christians ... not any *enthusiastic fervors* of spirit—not a firm *persuasion* that we are *elected* of God, and that *our names are written in the book of life.*

The movement toward denominationalism, secularism, and the impersonal God of the Deists set in motion a counter-trend. A wrathful, personal God who made the righteous prosper and sent the lightning to strike down the evil-doer was as comforting as He was awful, and ordinary men and women did not abandon Him easily. Such a God guarded heaven's portals. Yet men were avaricious for the things of this world and the gentle, easygoing God of the Deists and liberal theologians understood the ways of the world better than fierce old Jehovah. Heaven or the world? This God or that? Men tried vainly to decide or reconcile and tensions built up, particularly in New England where so many ministers emulated Jeremiah the Prophet in threatening a holocaust from the Lord if men did not reform, and inventing a perfect past—the founding years—to hold up as an example to their sinful present. And tensions of a religious nature combined with other tensions inherent in the colonial milieu. We have noted the crowding of older communities. Sons, waiting for land, were forced to put off marriage. Brought up on the comparatively lavish landholdings of their fathers, they had to settle for less than their expectations. Men who moved from old communities to find land in new areas were choosing (under duress) the discomfort of the unknown over the comfort of the known, an uncomfortable rootlessness over the comfort of family and a sense of belonging. We have noted the tendency for social lines to harden, but we must note too that while the tradition and examples of social mobility inspired expectations, the monopolization of high places by a few and the stagnation in lower places by others meant frustration for the latter.

Religious and secular tensions led directly to such outbreaks as the Massachusetts witch hunts of 1692-1693. The Devil and his imps were abroad in and around Salem —did not witnesses testify to the "black man" seen whispering in Martha Corey's ear? Before it ended twenty "witches" were executed, two more died in prison, one man was pressed to death, some 150 were jailed.

More importantly, the tensions led men into the enthusiasm of religious revivalism. Here and there, from the turn of the seventeenth to the eighteenth centuries, some ministers sought to reinvigorate the failing Jehovah in a variety of ways, ultimately attempting to drive men to Him by threatening the pains of Hell in the most vehement terms. Their efforts precipitated outbursts of enthusiastic religion—as Solomon Stoddard did periodically in Northampton, Massachusetts, and later his grandson Jonathan Edwards. Edwards was, however, more than a mere hell-fire-and-damnation preacher; a subtle theologian, fully aware of Europe's intellectual achievements, he attempted to bring the "new learning" to the support of old theology in erudite expositions of *The Modern Prevailing Notions of... Freedom of the Will*—there was no such thing he argued—and *The Great Christian Doctrine of Original Sin Defended.* In New Jersey and Pennsylvania, ministers such as Theodore Frelinghuysen and Gilbert Tennent preached of the old Jehovah. Throughout the first four decades of the eighteenth century local revivals flared up and died away. When, in the late 1730s, evangelists from England's Methodist movement—most notably George Whitefield—appeared preaching a doctrine of sin and repentance, conversion and salvation, revivalism swept the colonies in periodic waves, the "Great Awakening" as it is called.

This first awakening (there would be others in the national period) soon subsided. Men scrambled to Jehovah, perhaps found Him, then drifted away again. But in the process of the Awakening, as some men followed the evangelists and others followed more regular clerics, congregations and denominations split, furthering the fragmentation of American religion. And as men regularly challenged ministers reluctant to preach the direct religion of the evangelists, they undermined still further the authority of the clergy and of formal religion itself. Above all, however, insofar as religion bulwarked and rationalized the social order—the sublimation of the individual to the well being of the whole society, the division of society into rich and poor, rulers and ruled—the Awakening's challenge to religion was a challenge to the social order. The authority over the individual of king, governor, and the natural order of society itself were, on the very eve of the Revolution, weakened by the denigration of the authority of ministers and of formal churches which accompanied the godly fervor of the Awakening.

6.
Government and Politics

To THE COLONIAL of the eighteenth century, the government of his province was of paramount importance. King George was his sovereign, London a distant seat of empire, but his government at Boston, Hartford, Philadelphia, or Williamsburg had an integrity, even a sovereignty, of its own. His government was tied to England, true; the crown in England was an ultimate authority, and governors sent from England (in all but Connecticut and Rhode Island) were integral parts of the governmental structure. But the colonial nevertheless assumed that in an empire of many parts, the parts were self-regulating. The assumption was primarily pragmatic. To the average man the provincial capital was as far as his political horizon reached; to greater men, the capital was the primary arena of politics, politics was a way to power, and power both a reward and a source of wealth. The assumption was, moreover, a product of a historical process which began with the very first settlements of the seventeenth century.

107

The Origins of Self-Government

Neither the English monarchy nor the English Parliament planted colonies in the American wilderness, a fact of vital importance when we consider the beginnings of self-government. Individuals in search of profit, reformers and religious figures in search of a place in which dreams could become reality—these were, as we have seen, the men who supplied the drive to organize and fund the opening up of first one, then another, area. The investment of their time and money, or the requirements of their dreams for reformed societies, led them to insist on control of their own ventures. They obtained royal charters from the crown which recognized the private nature of the various colonial efforts and gave the backers—whether joint-stock organizations such as the Virginia or Massachusetts Bay companies or single individuals such as Lord Baltimore—the power to regulate their own affairs and govern their settlements with little reference to monarch or nation. There were limitations on their powers; they were not to establish any "laws, statutes, ordinances and directions ... contrary to the laws of this our realm of England." But as historian Charles M. Andrews has written, "in reality these settlements were not colonies; they were private estates."

Self-government was, therefore, inherent in English colonization from the beginning, but only in the sense of the commercial companies or proprietors being allowed to govern, not the right of the actual settlers to participate in the governance of their own affairs. Still, it was a step and one followed quickly by a second. Commercial organizations and proprietors very early discovered that ambitious, acquisitive Englishmen would not venture their lives and fortunes in the New World without some say in their own government, that they were as unwilling to settle overseas while their affairs were subject to control by private persons as the private persons were unwilling to involve themselves in overseas projects subject to control by the state. Of necessity, therefore, the private persons to whom the crown had given powers of self-regulation came to share those powers with the settlers themselves.

The process is clearly seen with regard to Virginia. In the founding of Jamestown in 1607 London merchants supplied the capital and organization in anticipation of profits but the crown retained control of the settlement. Pressure from the merchants, combined with economic failure and near chaos in the settlement, resulted in a change in 1609. The Virginia Company was formally chartered and empowered to appoint a governor and all officers for the settlement and to lay down either directly or through its officers the rules and regulations by which the colonists were to live. For a time—roughly 1610-1618—the Company sent military men to the colony to rule, establishing an authoritarian regime in which the settlers had absolutely no voice. The regime succeeded in stabilizing the situation in Virginia. But it maintained a communal economy in which all worked for the benefit of all and took food from a common warehouse—a system anathema to acquisitive Englishmen. Its edicts all too often seemed to the settlers detrimental rather than efficacious, as when the governor ordered that no man plant tobacco without planting an equivalent amount of grain. And its bad reputation in England tended to dissuade would-be settlers. As a result the colony failed to prosper and grow; it displayed "the quiet primness of a corpse"—very well laid out but not alive. The regime was collapsing under pressure from leading settlers themselves when the Company finally realized the futility of the effort along these lines. In 1619, while doing away with the last remnant of the communal economy, the Company directed the establishment of a representative body of the settlers, transferring to this body (the House of Burgesses) a part of the right of self-regulation which the crown, by charter, had earlier given to the Company.

There is somewhat the same progression in Massachusetts Bay. Again, the Massachusetts Bay Company chartered in 1629 was given broad powers of self-regulation. But when John Winthrop and his Puritan fellows contemplated settling on the Company's lands, they agreed to go only if control of the Company were transferred to themselves. The transfer effected, they carried Company, charter, and all (the "home office" so to speak) to the New World. Of course, the transfer of control had been from English merchants to a small coterie of leading figures of the 1630 migration who were also members of the Company. Consequently government in the Bay area was, during the first few years, conducted by those few. But the exclusion from government of the great bulk of the adult males was readily discerned as a problem. Membership in the Company was consequently expanded (membership being the equivalent of the right to vote in the affairs of the Company) to include all upstanding, godly men who applied, the criterion of upstanding-and-godly being church affiliation. The very term for a member or shareholder in the Company—"freeman"—became synonymous with "voting citizen." Gradually, too, in the earliest years, a representative legislative body came into existence.

Virginia and Massachusetts Bay were in a way precedents for the future and all later colonial charters required that the exclusive grant of self-regulation given the charterees be shared with the actual colonists. Conforming to this requirement, legislative bodies made their appearance in Maryland, the Carolinas, Pennsylvania, the Jerseys, and elsewhere. Even with the appearance of royal government, first in Virginia when the crown in 1624 assumed control of the bankrupt Company, the delegation to the colonists of a voice in their own affairs was continued. Thus, while the crown (rather than the Company) appointed the governors and advisory councils, the representative House of Burgesses, although its sessions were interrupted, remained a part of the government. It had proven indispensable.

In such an off-handed way did the beginnings of self-government come to the colonies: the monarch granting self-regulation to private persons backing colonies and the private persons, finding it necessary to make colonization by Englishmen successful, sharing their powers of self-regulation with the settlers. Yet it was still but a beginning, vague and ill-defined. On the one hand, the relationship between local governments in the colonies and the government in London was unclear. On the other, the relationship within each colony between the representative legislature and what we can term the "executive" (be that executive the Puritan leadership, a proprietor, or a royal governor) was muddy. Much of the political history of the colonies to the 1760s revolved around efforts to define these two sometimes intertwined relationships.

Empire and the Tensions of a New Society

The establishment of a tradition of self-regulation *vis-à-vis* London was furthered during the mid-seventeenth century decades by the preoccupation of the English crown with affairs at home—the Civil War and Cromwellian interlude. During England's troubles the colonies went very much their own way.

Massachusetts Bay, evincing all the attributes of sovereignty, declared herself neutral in England's internal war and acted for all the world like an independent nation. The terms of her purely commercial charter were violated time and time again as she banished and even executed her enemies. Those colonies which sprang up around Massachusetts—New Haven, the Connecticut River towns, Rhode Island—had not a wisp of English sanction until long after their foundation. The New England governments of Massachusetts, Plymouth, New Haven, and the River towns formed an extra-legal alliance (the New England Confederation), declared offensive war against the nearby Pequot Indians (Massachusetts' charter allowed her only to defend herself), made peace and argued about the spoils, conducted independent negotiations with a foreign power (the Dutch at New Amsterdam) and entered into a treaty with that same nation (the Treaty of Hartford of 1650 establishing a boundary between English and Dutch settlements). And when England herself went to war with the Dutch in the 1650s, the New Englanders all but ignored the conflict.

Farther south, Maryland was wracked by its own civil wars as men seeking their personal aggrandizement, frequently under the cloak of religion, threw legality to the wind and resorted to force. In the 1640s Governor Leonard Calvert was ousted by a swashbuckling sea captain and a grasping Virginian; he won the government back only with the aid of the governor of Virginia. In the 1650s settlers in the Annapolis area, claiming that it violated their liberty of conscience as Christians, refused to swear an oath of fidelity to the proprietor which would have obligated them to pay for the lands they had taken up. Not until the Restoration was the tumult they provoked temporarily settled. In Virginia, the government declared for the king in the Civil War, but after making token surrender to Parliamentary agents in 1652 proceeded to set up a government in which the elected House of Burgesses ruled supreme, even to the extent of electing and removing governors at will.

What can be termed an era of "quasi-independence" came to a close in the years following the Restoration. Those in England involved in colonial trade, as we have seen, successfully pressed for legislation which would define the empire in commercial terms. The resulting Acts of Trade and Navigation required enforcement, however, and a well-defined relationship between colonial governments and the government at home. Investigations were set afoot, as in 1664 when a royal commission was sent to New England to look into charges of near-independent action. Royal officials (in addition to royal governors) made their appearance, charged with enforcing the various acts. In England attempts were made to set up some sort of central administration which would consolidate colonial affairs and act as a brake on colonial action—there having been no such group that amounted to anything in the early years. In 1675 the Lords of Trade, a subcommittee of the king's Privy Council, was established to advise that august body on colonial affairs.

We have already referred to the conjunction of English merchants and colonial officials which came to form a pressure group advocating extreme measures to force the colonials to a proper respect for the Acts of Trade and Navigation and a proper allegiance to England. The Lords of Trade, particularly their secretariat—paid and permanent secretaries and clerks whose entire career was the administration of the affairs of empire—became the focal point of this pressure group. The secretariat, together with men in other departments of the government, notably treasury and customs, and men like Edward Randolph, Robert Quary, Francis Nicholson, and Edmund Andros who went overseas as servants of the king in one capacity or another, constituted an emerging colonial bureaucracy. One might even say they constituted an "imperial clique," although the word "empire" did not have for them the aura that it has for us. Affected by the paranoia of the merchants, rebuffed by colonials clinging to old ways, aghast at the loose ties between England and Englishmen settled overseas, frequently men of military background with a strict sense of duty and loyalty to the monarchy, they gradually emerged as a potent force for reform.

With the bureaucracy leading the way, a concerted attempt was made to return to the king all the outstanding self-regulatory powers previously awarded to commercial companies and proprietors. In 1680 New Hampshire, originally a proprietary of the Mason family but most recently a fief of Massachusetts Bay, was transformed into a royal colony. In 1681 the Lords of Trade bitterly resisted Penn's efforts to obtain a charter. The charter was issued but Penn was given far less exclusive power than previous charterees. In 1682 the Lords defeated a move to establish a new proprietary colony in Florida on the grounds that it was not convenient for the king "to grant any further powers that might render the plantations less dependent on the crown." The next year, on the advice of the Lords, legal proceedings were begun to declare Massachusetts' charter vacant on the basis of the colony's having exceeded charter-imposed limitations, proceedings culminating in the revocation of the charter in 1684. The accession of the Duke of York as James II automatically ended the New York proprietary, New York becoming a royal colony.

The height of this effort was reached in 1685 when the charters of Connecticut and Rhode Island were to all intents and purposes suspended and the whole of New England fused into one grand "Dominion of New England," a royal government under Sir Edmund Andros which allowed the colonists a minimum of participation. There was to be no representative assembly, only Andros carrying out instructions from London and assisted by a royally-appointed deputy governor and council. New York and the Jerseys were subsequently joined to the Dominion; ultimately, it would seem, Pennsylvania and Maryland were to have been included.

England's actions during the twenty-nine years following the Restoration created tension, particularly in New England. Long before, in the 1630s, the leaders of Massachusetts Bay, when faced with a threat to their charter, had determined to fight rather than yield. Their determination had not been tested, however, for the threat had dissipated with the outbreak of England's troubles. During the years of quasi-independence, self-government had become, in the New England mind, a traditional right founded on the provisions of the charter. Yet the New Englanders were always Englishmen and proud of it; England itself was "home." England's actions after 1660 raised the basic question: How can our tie to home be reconciled with the right to govern ourselves? Are we, the New Englanders asked each other, but a mere colony or a commonwealth joined to England by a common king? If the former, how are our English liberties to be protected?

The liberties of our churches? What of our royal charter and the privileges it allows us? If the latter, wherein lies the tie to England? What is the nature of our obligation to a royal sovereign? And arguing these points without resolution, the New Englanders steered an erratic (and, to watching Englishmen, exasperating) course. The New Englanders quibbled—rejecting, in one instance, a communication signed by His Majesty's secretary "in the name" of the king because it was not signed by the king himself. They professed their loyalty and sent gifts to the monarch while finding reasons to deny that the king's servants had authority within their boundaries. And they split hairs, as when the Massachusetts Deputies, asserting their exclusive right to legislate for the colony, attempted to repass the Acts of Trade and Navigation as their own statutes, rather than Parliament's.

There was tension of another sort, too, less conscious, less public, but common to all the colonies, one ultimately entangled with that tension arising from the ill-defined relationship with England. The recreation of a hierarchic structure for society—that already described—was proceeding throughout the century. Fortunes were being laid down by acquisitive men, and these self-made men were continually striving for political position to match their economic position. The number of positions from which political power can be wielded are limited in any society, however, and in English America there were soon too few such positions for the number of men who sought them. There was, consequently, a continuing rivalry for positions of power among the colonials.

Already what can be termed a basic structure for colonial governments had evolved. A governor (elected in New England's chartered colonies, appointed by crown or proprietor elsewhere) served as chief executive, assisted by an elected or appointed council. Governor and council together served as a high judicial body as well, and when joined by an elected lower house (in all but New York where the ducal proprietor—James—disliked and disallowed popular representation) as the colony's legislature.

Within this structure men of wealth sought positions on the royal or proprietary councils or, in New England, the governorship itself. Those who achieved economic position only to find that there was no room for them at the top of the political ladder settled for positions in the lower houses of the legislature. Here they sought to make their lesser vantage point ever greater, becoming ardent supporters of legislative rights against fellow colonials above them as well as against crown or proprietor. The dichotomy in colonial ranks prompted bitter fights in the seventeenth century. In Massachusetts, for example, the House of Deputies snapped at the council throughout the 1630s and 1640s, gaining autonomy and a veto of legislation. Following the Restoration, the Deputies again fought the councillors, tending to uphold the "commonwealth" position against the "colony" position of the latter. In New York the absence, for most of the period of seventeenth-century English control, of a lower house made the competition for positions of power all the more bitter. Those who lost argued vehemently for a legislative body in which they could sit, while those who won positions around the governor formed a proprietary coterie, cautiously opposing a legislature. In Maryland the tension underlay the frequent violence of the years of quasi-independence and Restoration. Between 1652 and 1691 there were five rebellions; governorship and council positions were kicked about and held first by one side then another. In Virginia, the tension flared out in open rebellion when a young madcap, Nathaniel Bacon, taking advantage of an argument as to how best to meet a threat from the Indians, led an insurgency against Governor William Berkeley. Prominent Virginians took sides according to their standing with the governor. "Bacon's Rebellion" (1675-1676) was brutally quashed, but in its aftermath the lines reformed on the old basis—"ins" versus "outs," with the outs seizing upon the House of Burgesses as their vantage point. Even in newly settled Carolina the tension was beginning to show.

The creation of the Dominion of New England, although it involved only the northern colonies, increased everywhere the tensions arising both from the ill-defined relationship to England and from the internal political balance. On the one hand, the question of the relationship between England and the colonies was, in effect, answered by England in terms of an absolute dependence of the colonies upon their mother—an intolerable answer to the colonials, even though they did not have a precise definition of the relationship. The actions of the Dominion government in regard to defense and land titles were, moreover, such as to discredit England's answer, for Indian raids were not quelled and alodial land titles in New England were put into jeopardy by crown officials seemingly intent on substituting feudal tenures. On the other hand, the absence of a legislative body excluded from all positions of political power those most anxious for power. The resultant explosion—inherent in the situation—was precipitated by events in England, the "Glorious Revolution" of 1688.

In England the proclivity of the later Stuarts (Charles II and James II) to Catholicism and the pretensions particularly of James to absolutism had let to plotting, an invitation to James' Protestant daughter Mary and her husband William, Prince of Orange, to assume the throne, and rebellion as William landed at Torbay with 15,000 Netherlands soldiers. James' overthrow was quick and relatively easy. Rumors of these great happenings flew rapidly overseas. In Massachusetts early in 1689 the officials of the Dominion government were seized and imprisoned; William and Mary were proclaimed as England's sovereigns; agents were dispatched to plead for the restoration of the old charter. Connecticut, Rhode Island, Plymouth, and New Hampshire quietly resumed their separate existence and former governments. In New York, those without political power took advantage of the situation to declare for the new sovereigns to seize the government, Jacob Leisler, one of the "outs," assuming control as commander-in-chief of the militia in the resulting confusion. To the south, the

Maryland "outs" recognized William and Mary and organized a "Protestant Association" which defeated the governor and his followers and established itself as the government. In Virginia there was murmuring, but no overt action. In the Carolinas the "outs" formed factions—as they periodically did—which eventually resulted in the replacement of the governor.

The wave of rebellions brought to an end the Dominion of New England although it did not result in a complete restoration of old ways. What has been referred to as an imperial bureaucracy or clique remained to advise the new sovereigns as it had the old, and its advice was still the same: Tighten the reins of empire, strengthen the power of the crown abroad. Indeed, the potency of the clique increased in the years after 1696. The Act of Trade and Navigation of that year, in regularizing the colonial customs service and erecting colonial admiralty courts, established new empire offices in London, the incumbents of which more often than not gravitated into the imperial clique. The Lords Commissioners of Trade and Plantations (more commonly called the Board of Trade) organized in 1696 very quickly became a new and stronger focal point for the clique. Unlike the Lords of Trade which it replaced and whose secretariat it retained, the Board was divorced completely from the Privy Council. Half of its membership of sixteen constituted a "working body," eight men permanently employed and salaried, sitting regularly under their president to consider commercial and colonial matters. (The other eight were great officers of state and members of Parliament serving without pay and usually on an irregular basis.) Anything to do with the colonies came within the purview of the Board. It could investigate what it wanted, require reports from colonial officials, and advise any part of the government on colonial matters either on request or on its own initiative.

William and Mary on ascending the throne had no other recourse but to listen to the advice of the bureaucracy when colonial matters came up. Enemies assailed Penn (a long-time friend of James) and Baltimore (Catholic) and both Penn and Baltimore temporarily lost control of their provinces. Pennsylvania was soon restored to its proprietor, but the Baltimores did not regain control of Maryland until 1715; in both cases the proprietors found that they had less power after the period of royal control than before. Massachusetts' agents applying to the monarchs for the restoration of the old charter were refused; instead a new charter was granted (1691) by which Plymouth and Massachusetts Bay were joined together, the enlarged colony to be governed by a royally-appointed governor, a popularly elected lower house, and a council nominated by the house and appointed by the governor. Massachusetts grudgingly accepted.

As the seventeenth century closed and the eighteenth opened, the imperial clique pressed vigorously for a tightening of the fabric of empire. It sought the establishment of a standing army in the colonies, one maintained by taxes levied by Parliament and commanded by a "Captain General over all the plantations on the continent" to whom the governors would be subordinate, the commander and army charged not only with defending the colonies but with obtaining "by all possible means the entire, absolute, and immediate dependency" of the colonies on the crown. The Board solicited acts of Parliament which would annul all charters and erect uniform royal governments, or acts which would at least curtail charter rights. (The first was the "Reunification Bill" of 1701, ardently pleaded for by members of the Board and against by William Penn.) Failing in this, the Board pressed the crown to purchase or otherwise assume charter rights, successfully with regard to the Jerseys (1702) and the Carolinas (1729), almost successfully with regard to Pennsylvania. The Board argued that royal instructions to royal governors were binding upon the colonials, that what a governor was required by his instructions from London to obtain in the way of laws or revenues a colonial legislature was required to give. And when colonial legislatures refused this interpretation of instructions and, by with-holding all revenues, forced governors to their way of thinking, individual members of the clique urged that Parliament vote a permanent English-raised revenue to pay the salaries of the royal officials in America and so free those officials from reliance on colonial legislatures.

By virtue of the influence of the imperial clique, England still insisted that colony-mother country relations be defined in terms of colonial dependence. The colonials, however, tied to the tradition of self-regulation yet tied to England by an innate loyalty could neither wholeheartedly accept nor wholeheartedly reject such dependence. Among colonials, too, those without positions of power still contested with those who had power. In New York the colonial leaders ousted by Leisler and his followers gained the ear of the new governor sent by William and Mary. Leisler was executed for treason and for twenty years thereafter the colony was split between Leislerians and anti-Leislerians, each alternately gaining the favor of royal governors and seeking to quash their opponents.

Factionalism continued to build the power of the lower legislative houses, for in the lower houses those excluded from the highest positions built up their own importance. That revenues could, by virtue of charter provisions and royal instructions, be raised within the colonies only with the consent of the lower houses gave those houses the weapon they needed, and using this "power of the purse" they everywhere gathered power to themselves, nibbling constantly at the prerogatives of governors and councils. They reached out to assume control of executive officers and judges by assuming control of salaries, fee-schedules, and by insisting on their right to nominate incumbents, even to fix set terms of office in place of the traditional appointment "during the pleasure of His Majesty." Everywhere, too, the colonial houses constituted themselves "little parliaments," arguing that whatever powers *vis-à-vis* the crown the great Parliament in London had, they had *vis-à-vis* their governors. They built magnificent statehouses in Boston, Williamsburg, and elsewhere, and adopted the formality and symbolism of Westminster as the physical embodiments of their argument—the mace, for example, the presence of which symbolized that Parliament was in session.

If the rebellions themslves did not ease tensions, the tensions did ease in time. The same forces which were halting efforts to enforce the trade acts were operating in the political sphere. The influence of the Board of Trade and the imperial clique which it institutionalized waned as the eighteenth century progressed and the period of salutary neglect set in. It was inevitable. The Board's effectiveness depended upon the ability and willingness of other departments of the government to accept and act on its advice, for the Board had little real power of its own. Robert Walpole as first lord of the treasury (1715-1717, 1721-1742), his successor Henry Pelham (1743-1754), and Thomas Pelham, Duke of Newcastle as Secretary of State and Henry Pelham's successor in the treasury (to 1762)— such men tended to reject or ignore the Board. Ineffective, the Board's members lost interest; their meetings became irregular, their presidency a mere sinecure. Not until 1748, when the Earl of Halifax assumed the presidency, would the Board begin to come alive again.

With the near demise of the Board, the point of view it represented—absolute colonial dependence upon and control by England—was seldom pressed officially. Colonials were no longer required to choose between dependence and self-regulation. Indeed, they proceeded as if the problem had been resolved in favor of the latter and saw the empire as a happy union of self-regulating parts linked together by the person of the king and the commercial regulations of the Parliament.

The tensions created by the competition of "ins" and "outs" eased as well. For as the importance of the lower houses grew, men were relatively content with the power that a seat among the Deputies (in Massachusetts) or the Burgesses (in Virginia) or the Common House of Assembly (in South Carolina) afforded. And as society became less fluid in the eighteenth century, there were fewer new men of wealth seeking positions of political power. Yet the tensions did not disappear altogether. In 1763 a Marylander wrote that it was "impossible for all men to be in place, and those who are out will grumble and strive to thrust themselves in." The same year, James Otis of Massachusetts wrote of the world divided "between those who are discontented that have no power, and those who never think they can have enough." Factionalism still existed as political leaders combined and recombined on public issues and in pursuit of "places." But the violent factionalism of the seventeenth century ebbed and a sometimes sonorous, sometimes rancorous, but a generally peaceful legislative factionalism prevailed.

The Political Climate of the Eighteenth Century

James Otis, in writing disparagingly of men's quest for power, reflected both the actuality and the idea of eighteenth century politics. Colonial leaders sought power and condemned the seeking of power at one and the same time.

The root of the ambiguity lay in the structure of government. Colonial governments were, as they had been in the seventeenth century, compounded of governors, councils, and elected lower legislative houses. But events during the decades immediately before and after the turn of the century, primarily those inspired by the imperial clique, had augmented the power of the governors. There were fewer elected governors; in all but Rhode Island and Connecticut, the governors were proprietary or royal appointees. The theoretical powers of the governors were greater, indeed, greater even than those allowed the king in England, for in arguing absolute colonial dependence upon England, the imperial clique had conceived of the governors as the agents imposing that absolute dependence. And governors had more political offices at their disposal.

Every new act of Parliament in the seventeenth and early eighteenth century meant a new array of customs and fiscal, judiciary and executive officials to be appointed in the colonies by the governors. At the same time, however, the powers of the lower legislative houses had steadily risen. In essence, a fine balance of power between governors and lower houses had been established. Neither could operate without the support of the other. Governors could not perform their executive duties nor carry out instructions from crown or proprietors without legislative support; neither could legislators obtain public or private legislation without the approbation of governors. Governors, consequently, sought to build factions within the legislatures, buying support by the award of offices. And colonial legislators built factions within the lower houses in order that they might trade with the governor for offices for themselves and the governor's support of public and private legislation important to them.

The constant political jockeying inherent in this situation need not detain us. In some colonies relative stability was achieved. In Virginia and South Carolina colonial political leaders formed homogenous and integrated groups and from their positions in the legislatures forced a stable *modus vivendi* on their governors; in New Hampshire the royal governor built such a strong machine on the basis of patronage as to dominate the legislature and the colonial political leaders almost completely; in New York, Pennsylvania, and elsewhere equally strong legislative factions solidified around dominant personalities or families or on a sectional or religious basis, and alternated with each other in the favor of the governor. We must note, however, the anomaly of the colonial position inherent in the situation. Bartering legislative support for gubernatorial favor, colonial leaders had all the while to maintain the power of their legislatures against the governors (and against England, the ultimate authority). In essence, the colonial political figure, winning or losing in the day-to-day politics of his province—in the sense of winning or losing the favor of the governor—was always, in defense of his legislative power, in opposition to gubernatorial and English prerogatives.

That he was always in opposition explains the partiality of the colonial political figure for the literature of opposition emanating from England. There, much the same configuration of politics had appeared. The power of the monarch had, in the seventeenth and early eighteenth century, been circumscribed by that of Parliament—the House of Commons and the House of Lords. Leading figures of Parliament had become the king's principal secretaries, dominating the royal administration. But these great lords of state had turned around and, through the use of patronage, come to dominate Parliament itself, in

CENTRAL ELEMENTS IN POLITICAL LIFE

A Colonial Capitol
The capitol in Williamsburg, seat of the House of Burgesses

Colonial Williamsburg Collection, Williamsburg, Virginia

effect monopolizing all power to themselves. Those devoid of power in this arrangement resorted to print and, building on an amalgam of current political theories, constructed a negative theory of politics.

The starting point of the opposition's negative theory was a political philosophy common to all politically-minded Britishers—including those in the colonies—one

A COLONIAL GOVERNOR
Jonathan Belcher, Governor of Massachusetts, 1730–1741

epitomized in the writings of John Locke which had been used to rationalize the 1688 revolution. Locke himself was not original; he merely crystallized earlier statements as to political theory, particularly in the second of his *Two Treatises of Government.*

Briefly, and put too simply, Locke argued that originally men existed in a state of nature, enjoying perfect liberty "to order their actions and dispose of their possessions and persons" as they would "without asking leave, or depending upon the will of any other man." But liberty was not license. "The state of nature has a law of nature to govern it," Locke wrote. Men cannot destroy themselves or, without reason, their possessions, nor can they transgress upon the "life, liberty, and estate" of others. If they did so, every other man had a natural right to defend the law of nature by punishing the criminal and taking reparations from those who injured him. This natural state was an uncomfortable one, however. All men being kings, every man equal, "and the greater part no strict observers of equity and justice," the individual's enjoyment of life, liberty, and estate was "very unsafe, very insecure." Consequently men had combined in societies. By agreement or compact—sometimes explicit, more often implicit in their choosing to live with others in a community—they had surrendered a certain amount of their natural liberty to the community or commonwealth in return for group protection of their quiet enjoyment of what remained. They had agreed to surrender equality for the stability of an ordered hierarchy, to abide by the will of the majority of the community rather than their own will. They had subjected themselves to the authority of a government of society's devising which could put the law of nature in statute form and exert power to enforce it. They had even consented to give a necessary support to government by surrendering to it a part of their property in the form of taxes. But government created to protect the individual in his enjoyment of life, liberty, and estate was automatically limited. It could not violate the purposes for which it was created, could not take its subjects' lives or deprive them of their liberty or property capriciously or for any other reason than the common good.

Yet, stressed the opposition writers, government would inevitably attempt to exceed its purposes, for governments were compounded of men and power, and men were inherently corruptible by power. All history demonstrated this proposition, for all history was the story of men fighting for their liberty against some sort of tyranny. Innately "voracious like the grave," "restless and selfish," any man once tasting power over other men "can never have enough" but would use what power he had to gain more power. Therefore government must be kept as minimal as possible—the less government was allowed to do, the less power there would be for corruptible men to wield. Power must be diffused in government so that no man had overly much, and one man's power was balanced and checked by another's. Above all, men in government must be constantly watched by public-spirited citizens for they would just as constantly conspire to enlarge their power at the expense of men's liberties. Such men "lie under great temptations," for out of "the infirmities and corruption of human nature" they are led "to prefer their own private interest to that of the community ... wicked ministers have exerted their endeavors, in all ages, to abridge the liberties of the people and wrest the laws to the punishment of their fellow-subjects."

In the English context, the opposition held, again in common with all politically minded Britishers, that the British government was, theoretically, the finest ever evolved, a well-balanced compound of monarch, Lords, and Commons, each guarding the liberty of an estate of the realm—king, aristocracy, and the people—by acting independently to watch and check the corrupting influence of power upon the others. Liberty was better preserved from power in this government than it had ever been in any other. Yet the balance was tenuous and the great lords of state were conspiring to overturn it. Having

captured the monarch, they were inveigling "the *deputies*
of the people" in Commons to depart from their duty of
watching and checking, offering honors, titles, prefer-
ments, and bribes. "Some" in Parliament "are persuaded
to prostitute themselves for the lean reward of hopes and
promises; and others, more senseless than all of them, have
sacrificed their principles and consciences to a set of party
names without any meaning, or the vanity of appearing in
favor at court." If successful, the great lords of state would
destroy all liberty by embarking on costly wars, by maintaining a standing army ostensibly to protect the people
but in reality to dominate them, by building a public debt
and enacting grinding taxes to service the debt and pay
the army—classic ways, as history as diverse as that of the
Roman Nero and the Turkish *bashaws* shows, by which
tyranny had waged its constant war on liberty.

Among colonial political leaders, there was also pride in
the British balance and the preservation of British liberty.
The pride was transferred to the provinces and there was
pride in the provincial balance between governors and
legislators and the preservation of provincial liberty. But
innately in opposition, the politically minded colonial im-
bibed the negative theory of politics of the British opposition. Hence, even while playing politics, while bartering
with his governor and trading legislative influence for an
office at the bestowal of the governor, even while pro-
claiming that liberty was best preserved under the British
government and its colonial reflection, the colonial was
suspicious—of the politics he was playing, of opposing factions for the governor's favor, of the governor, of the British authority which lay behind the governor and was, if
the British opposition was to be believed, in danger of
imbalance by virtue of great lords of state grown too powerful. The rhetoric of opposition sprang readily to the
colonial's lips. Thus a New York writer of 1734 wrote that
"there have been ... [governors] as very bashaws as ever
were sent from Constantinople; and there have not been
wanting under each of their administrations, persons the

dregs and scandal of human nature who have kept in with them, and used their endeavors to enslave their fellow subjects." A Boston pamphleteer noted in 1757 that "too great a number of placemen and pensioners [sit] in Parliament." "Will not . . . a noble public spirit fire us with an honest zeal in this part of the world to look about us and inquire if there have been any such among us who have been influenced by posts of honor and profit to vote and act too much as men in power would have them?" And Maryland's Charles Carroll, after visiting England in the 1750s and observing "the bribes, and the smiles of corruption and arbitrary ministers [of state]," wrote that liberty could not last much longer in England; corruption had proceeded too far and been so misused as to threaten "immediate ruin and already to have left to the people little more than the appearance of liberty."

Rulers and Ruled

The politics of the colonial world was dominated by the wealthy of the colonial society. Those who served on the governors' councils, as leaders in the lower houses of the legislatures, who won appointment to major public offices, were from the greatest families of the particular province —the wealthiest, the most prominent socially, the most successful in the quest for the governors' favor. Those who held local office and who made up the bulk of the membership of the lower houses were from families less wealthy and socially acceptable, but nevertheless prominent in their local areas as the others were prominent in the whole of a colony. This domination of government by the wealthy has led many to write of a "colonial aristocracy" as though there were a ruling class separate and apart from the populace in general. The phrase is an unhappy one, however, for it ignores the compatibility between rulers and ruled which prevailed in colonial society.

Political leadership everywhere proceeded from a popular base, even the most prominent men in effect winning their right to play the politics of the colonial capital by first winning election in their locality. The suffrage was, as it was in England, limited to men of property; even in Massachusetts the original limitation of the suffrage to members of the church had broken down toward the end of the seventeenth century, replaced by property qualifications. But in the colonies, property sufficient to meet the suffrage requirements was more easily obtained than in England. More people proportionately could vote in America than in England. Historians have calculated the suffrage rate in some areas to be as high as ninety per cent of the adult male population, exclusive of slaves and Indians. The election day scene was common everywhere: a carnival atmosphere as men talked, drank, traded—using the election day holiday for fun and business; the candidates' friends circulating, asking for support of their particular man, inviting voters to try the beer (or whiskey) and meats which their man had provided for all; the moment culminating for the voter when he stepped up to the sheriff impressively seated at a long table, the candidates seated about him.

Sheriff: "Mr. Blair, who do you vote for?"
Blair: "John Marshall."
Marshall, perhaps rising and offering his hand:
     "Your vote is appreciated, Mr. Blair."
Sheriff: "Who do you vote for, Mr. Buchanan?"
Buchanan: "For John Clopton."
Clopton: "Mr. Buchanan, I shall treasure that vote in my memory.
     It will be regarded as a feather in my cap forever."

Of course, both Marshall and Clopton would inevitably be men of wealth and standing in the community. Men of lesser worth occasionally ran for office but were generally defeated. The pattern of thought of the time was such that the generality expected the gentlemen to undertake public office, that men or families who had profited within the society should give the society their time and effort in governing in exchange. And the prominent men and families deemed it, for their part, both a right and a duty to serve.

Moreover, there was a trust in men of high degree on the part of men of low, the latter deferring to the judgement and knowledge of the former. It does not follow from this trusting attitude, however, that the colonial generality, having elected men to office, had no interest in what those men did. There was an intense and continuing awareness of the affairs of government insofar as government affected the individual directly.

The greatest interest was quite naturally in local government, for that touched the everyday life of the citizen to the greatest degree. Local government regulated the individual's economic activity; in local courts the individual sought justice; and from local officials he expected protection from the lawless. Town selectmen and county justices, consequently, worked under a public spotlight, and common folk were not hesitant about making their views known. On the higher level, the government in Williamsburg, Boston, or Philadelphia was a political troposphere which directly affected the generality only occasionally. From the capital the individual solicited by petition redress of grievances unresolvable on the local level; to the capital he remonstrated when no level of government satisfied him. At times, when events or enactments in the capital adversely affected a locality, the generality reacted by turning out the elected gentlemen in the lower house and electing new men (albeit they chose new men from among the local gentlemen). Or they resorted to outright violence. Thus in Pennsylvania, in 1763, mobs (the "Paxton Boys") erupted and marched on Philadelphia protesting what they considered the too gentle Indian policy of the government in the capital; in North and South Carolina, in the late 1760s, violence flared (the "Regulator" movement) when western localities felt aggrieved by the lack of effective law enforcement and the malpractices of local officials.

Nevertheless, deference on the part of the generality toward the gentlemen who ruled was the prevailing order. And the trust that the generality had in the gentry was to stand in good stead in the Revolution, when political leaders were to warn the people that provincial liberties were at stake. "You assert that there is a fixed intention to invade our rights and privileges," Virginians told an elected representative in 1774. "We own that we do not see this clearly, but since you assure us that it is so, we believe the fact. . . . We confide in you, and are ready to support you in every measure you shall think proper to adopt."

7.
Empire and Revolution

 I F, LIKE SOME omnipotent and time-free bird, we could soar above the colonial world of the mid-eighteenth century, peering down and into the minds of its dominant Anglo-Americans as well as into their houses, churches, and statehouses, we would see a world of things, institutions, and ideas which was almost but not quite English. The first colonists had set out to construct a "little England." What had eventuated was a physical environment bearing only a resemblance to the English countryside and a society which, while appearing English, was in reality something quite different. In economics, the structure of land, labor, and society, in politics and religion, there were differences large and small between the two cultures.

In other areas—areas beyond the scope of a short narrative such as this—we could discern distinctions. The language of the Anglo-American reflected to an extent the polyglot nature of the colonial experience in that it was an amalgam of English dialects with a sprinkling of Indian and African words and borrowings from a variety of European languages. The structure of the family had changed, although historians are only now exploring the subtleties of the transformation. There was a greater interest in popular education than in England and Europe. In the beginning, men and women in the wilds had been conscious of the danger that their children would grow up wild, particularly in New England where education was stressed for religious reasons, while in the eighteenth century the virtue of an educated citizenry was beginning to be recognized. In the absence of any other social organ undertaking the task, the state acted; the notion of free, public education was implanted, together with the embryonic thought that society owed everyone the ability to read and write.

The list of shifts and changes differentiating England and America is almost infinite. It is enough to recognize that they were differentiated.

A New Man, Yet Proud Briton

Already a few men were assuming that there was something to the word "American" other than an easy adjective to distinguish "the American colonies of Great Britain" from her other colonies. "What, then, is the American, this new man?" a French observer, St. John de Crèvecoeur, asked at the end of the colonial period:

He is an American, who leaving behind him all his ancient prejudices and manners, receives new ones from the new mode of life he has embraced, the new government he obeys, and the new rank he holds. . . . Americans are the western pilgrims, who are carrying along with them that great mass of arts, sciences, vigor, and industry which began long since in the east; they will finish the great circle. . . . The American is a new man, who acts upon new principles; he must therefore entertain new ideas, and form new opinions. From involuntary idleness, servile dependence, penury, and useless labor, he has passed to toils of a very different nature, rewarded by ample subsistence.—This is an American.

Nathaniel Ames of Boston foresaw more changes in the future of America, waxing eloquent in his almanac of 1758:

The curious have observed, that the progress of human literature (like the sun) is from the east to the west; thus has it traveled through Asia and Europe, and now is arrived at the eastern shore of *America.* . . . Arts and sciences will change the face of nature in their tour from hence over the Appalachian mountains to the western ocean. . . . Rocks will disclose their hidden gems, and the inestimable treasures of gold and silver [will] be broken up. Huge mountains of iron ore are already discovered and vast stores are reserved for future generations. This metal, more useful than gold and silver, will employ millions of hands, not only to form the martial sword, and peaceful share, alternately, but an infinity of utensils improved by the exercise of art, and handicraft amongst men. . . . Shall not then those vast quarries, that team with mechanic stone—those for structure be piled into greater cities—and those for sculpture into statues to perpetuate the honor of renowned heroes; even those who shall now save their country. *O! Ye unborn inhabitants of America! Should this page escape its destined conflagration at the year's end, and these alphabetical letters remain legible when your eyes behold the sun after he has rolled the seasons round for two or three centuries more, you will know that in* Anno Domini 1758, *we dreamed of your times.*

Ames' exuberance was exceptional, however. The "new man" who had made his appearance in the world was more easily recognized by foreigners like Crèvecoeur than by the Americans themselves. In effect the new man did not recognize himself as such until the trauma of revolution overtook him.

For the Anglo-American colonists were, at mid-eighteenth century, proud Britons. Philadelphia's Francis Hopkinson—later he would serve in the Continental Congress, sign the Declaration of Independence, lampoon the British troops in his hilarious "Battle of the Kegs," and design the American flag for Betsy Ross to sew—celebrated the second capture of French Louisbourg in 1758:

> *At length 'tis done! the glorious conflict's done!*
> *And* British *valour has the conquest won!*
> Success *our arms, our heroes,* Honor *crowns,*

And Louisbourg an English *monarch owns....*

Hopkinson was reflecting the strong link which bound the colonies to Great Britain, the umbilical cord, if you will, connecting the child America to the parent. We have here stressed the deviation of the Anglo-American from his English origins. Yet this colonial felt more keenly what remained common in culture, history, heritage, and language. All felt themselves bound with the British under a common sovereign and gloried in their common liberty, although some feared that liberty was waning in Britain herself. All felt secure within a world-girdling empire.

Never prior to 1763 was this umbilical cord on the verge of breaking. True, colonial political leaders had objected when Britain interfered in the domestic affairs of their colony—as when Parliament struck down a Massachusetts land bank scheme in the 1740s. And from their provincial view of things, the colonists had taken offense at decisions in London which sublimated particular interests to the demands of empire—as they did in 1748 when, at the conclusion of one of the recurrent wars with France, London returned the French fortress of Louisbourg which the Massachusetts militia had captured. The treaty prompted this brief (but perhaps apocalyptical) soliloquy in Massachusetts:

Three thousand miles of water is a long way for parental ties to reach. The umbilical cord is stretched a trifle thin. The peacemakers at Aix-la-Chapelle are not endeavoring to strengthen it.... The mother country, you were pleased to call her. Shall we say—I am aware ... of straining my metaphor. Shall we say the child America is about to be abruptly weaned?

Such talk was only talk, however. The umbilical cord held strong and firm until 1763. The date is crucial. For after 1763 there was very little chance that the colonies could remain in the empire. In that year the Treaty of Paris marked a culmination of the great wars for empire between England and France. And American political leaders began to discern what they considered a departure from traditional imperial policy on the part of Britain, one which they conceived had as its aim the destruction of their political liberties.

The Wars for Empire

The expansion of western Europe in the sixteenth and seventeenth centuries had spread Europe's wars over the face of the globe. Trade routes had become battlegrounds, outposts and colonies pawns in a series of vast power struggles. Without recognizing the fact—for Europe's kings and princes thought that they were fighting for this bit of territory or that successor to a throne—the European powers were fighting for the domination of the world.

Even before England's American colonies were founded, Portugal and Spain had lost their bids for world supremacy. The colonial effort itself and their participation in European conflicts had robbed them of their vitality. Spain for a short time actually had swallowed Portugal whole. But Spain lost the long, dragging conflict with the Netherlands—the Netherlands' eighty-year war for independence—while England, in defeating the Spanish Armada in 1588, symbolically divested the Spanish monarch of his suzerainty over the seas. France, the Netherlands, and England began planting New World colonies despite Spanish pretensions to the whole of the American continents. Some strength was left in Spain, true, and Spain was a factor in the European power balance throughout the colonial period. Spanish and Portuguese possessions still girdled the world, but both Spain and Portugal were declining powers.

The struggles for empire in which England's continental colonies were involved were those between the Netherlands and England and between England and France.

In the seventeenth century England and the Netherlands were the leading competitors for world dominion. This was the golden age of that tiny nation of dikes and windmills. Her artists—Rubens, Rembrandt—were the world's finest. Her cities were world capitals. Her ships sailed every sea. And her merchants ruled an empire as broad as the times allowed, one which spanned the oceans from the Hudson and Delaware to the Cape of Good Hope, India, the East Indies, China, and Japan. But there was simply not enough country behind those dikes to maintain the position which brave seamen and energetic merchants had won. A mother country had to contribute something more than leadership to an empire. It had to send out men and supplies; it had to be able to defend its possessions with a strong navy; and it had to have the internal resources to withstand the buffeting which it inevitably received from jealous European neighbors.

The Netherlands did not have these things, hence its decline was foreseeable. France pressed against her on the continent; England pressed her at sea. Under Cromwell the first of three Anglo-Dutch wars was fought (1652-1654), with indecisive results. Under Charles II the conflict was continued (1665-1667 and 1672-1674). The plucky Dutch were not downed easily. In 1667 the Dutch fleet entered the Thames, burned three British men-of-war anchored in the safety of the river, towed away the *Royal Charles* (England's flagship), and momentarily won mastery of the English Channel; even in 1674 the Dutch home fleet was more than a match for England's. But the ravages of war on land (French invasion countered only by opening the dikes) and the loss of overseas outposts (including the Hudson and Delaware valleys) spelled the end of Dutch and the beginning of English supremacy on the ocean.

All the while France had been building a colonial empire. Well before England turned to the New World, Frenchmen had challenged Spain's pretensions in America, attempting unsuccessfully to settle along the Florida coast in the sixteenth century, settling Port Royal in what is now Nova Scotia in 1605 and Quebec in 1608. French expansion was desultory, however, and Anglo-French rivalry only sporadic until the triumph of French

absolutism, personified in Louis XIV, in the 1660s. Louis'
finance minister, Jean-Baptiste Colbert, devised and put
into operation a four-part system of empire: France would
serve as the heart of empire, supplying leadership, capital,
manufactured goods, and merchant services to the parts;
French islands in the West Indies would supply raw
materials—sugar, tobacco, indigo, cotton, dyewoods and
the like—to French industry and commerce; French slave
stations in Africa would supply the Negro labor needed in
the islands; French Canada, supplying furs to France,
would more importantly supply the Indies with foodstuffs
and lumber.

France's rise in Europe under Louis XIV and her rapid
emergence as a world power—eventually her ships pene-
trated the Indian Ocean to compete with England for the
trade which first the Portuguese, then the Dutch, had
dominated—would automatically have thrown her into
conflict with Great Britain. But the process was speeded
in 1688. The Glorious Revolution which saw the ouster of
the Stuarts, who had generally pursued a French policy in
Europe's power politics, saw too the advent of William
and Mary. Mary was of the English royal house, but William was of the Netherlands. The Netherlands and France
being enemies, William, now England's king, brought England into their conflict as ally to the Dutch. In the process, although the Netherlands could not regain the world
paramountcy she had lost to England, France could be
thwarted of the paramountcy she sought.

From 1689 to 1713 Anglo-French warfare was almost
continuous. In Europe the powers fought the War of the
League of Augsburg (1689-1697) and the War of the Spanish Succession (1702-1713); the American counterparts
were "King William's War" and "Queen Anne's War." To
monarchs and ministers the European conflicts were the
more vital and little in the way of money, soldiers, and
ships was expended overseas. Consequently in America
the wars were but a series of raids and counter-raids as
English and French dueled through their Indian allies—

the Iroquois of the Mohawk Valley allied with the English, most of the rest with the French. Occasionally Englishmen marched north along the upper Hudson, Lake George, Lake Champlain, and the Richelieu River—a time-honored invasion path for both sides—in an attempt to strike at the heartland of French Canada. Twice the New Englanders launched expeditions against French Nova Scotia, capturing Port Royal in 1690 only to see it returned to France in the Treaty of Ryswick (1697), capturing it again in 1710. To the south, Frenchmen on the lower Mississippi, Spaniards (allied with the French in the second war) in Florida, and Englishmen in Carolina sent their Indian allies against each other with indecisive results.

The Treaty of Utrecht of 1713 inaugurated a long truce, broken finally when English merchants, anxious to extend their trade in the Caribbean, forced a reluctant government to go to war with Spain in 1739. The conflict was a pathetic comedy from beginning to end. To force the government's hand and whip up popular and Parliamentary support, the war-party paraded master mariner Robert Jenkins and his severed ear before the House of Commons. How had he lost the ear? At the hands of a captain of the Spanish *guardacosta* who "tore [it] off . . . bidding him carry it to his king, and tell him they would serve him in the same manner should an opportunity offer." Few realized that the incident was seven years old or asked how the ear displayed to the House could be so well preserved. The country was mad for war, and when a Parliamentary back-bencher, Captain Edward Vernon, boasted that he could take the Spanish bastion of Porto Bello in Panama, headquarters of the *guardacostas*, with only six ships, popular feeling was such that the government had to let him try. Unfortunately he was spectacularly successful. Given more ships and an army, including an American-raised regiment, he was sent against Cartagena, the principal Caribbean port of the Spanish Main. But while Porto Bello had been unprepared, Cartagena was not. The 170 sails of the fleet, 15,000 seamen, and 9,000 soldiers— the largest force ever sent into western waters—failed disastrously as a result of the Spanish defense, arguments between British soldiers and sailors, and tropical disease. The "War of Jenkins' Ear" fizzled, then merged with a larger Anglo-French conflict, the War of the Austrian Succession (1740-1748), known in America as "King George's War," in which New Englanders under William Pepperrell took Louisbourg, the Cape Breton fortress built by the French after the loss of Port Royal to defend the entrance to the St. Lawrence. In negotiating the treaty of Aix-la-Chapelle, however, England returned Louisbourg in order to regain French conquests elsewhere. Aix was, as Ryswick had been, merely a truce, and the conflict resumed in 1754.

All previous contests had begun in Europe and spread to America; the new one, however, spread to Europe from America where French and English pretensions in mid-America finally came into direct contact. Already in the seventeenth century the Great Lakes had been a French canal. Along the chain of lakes French *coureurs de bois* traveled west in search of friendly Indians and furs, then southward, portaging from the lakes to the rivers flowing into the Mississippi. The first portages had been far to the west, but gradually the French had opened new portages to shorten the distance. Following the Treaty of Aix-la-Chapelle they began opening a route from Presque Isle on Lake Erie to the Allegheny and Ohio rivers, building a line of forts both to defend the passage and demarcate their own sphere of influence from that of the English. At the same time, however, Virginia Indian traders and land speculators, organized in 1747 as the Ohio Company, were moving into the area of the Monongahela and Ohio rivers. Virginians and Frenchmen began racing for that point where the Monongahela joins the Allegheny to form the Ohio—the "golden triangle" where present-day Pittsburgh stands. The Virginians won the race but before their fort was completed a superior force of French and Indian allies appeared and sent the Virginians packing. Virginia's governor sent twenty-two year old George Washington with a small force to oust the French, but Washington lost his first battle (Great Meadow), withdrew to a crude stockade (Fort Necessity), and subsequently lost

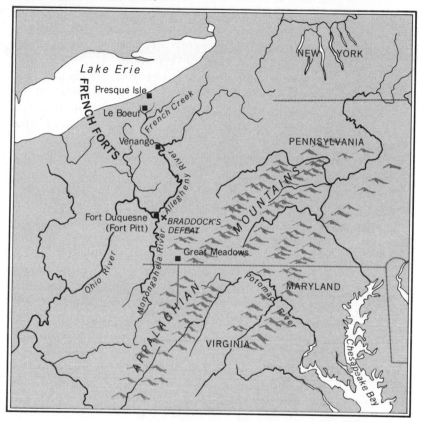

the whole campaign as the French surrounded him and forced his surrender.

As the French proceeded to build Fort Duquesne at the golden triangle, Virginia appealed to England for aid. The government, anxious to avoid a general war, decided on limited and undeclared war. Two regiments under General Edward Braddock would take Fort Duquesne and check the French on the Ohio; another force under William Johnson of New York would clear the French from Lake Champlain, where they were ensconced at Crown Point, dominating the traditional invasion path between the Hudson and St. Lawrence. Still another force under Governor William Shirley of Massachusetts would take Fort Niagara, a major link between French Canada and the portages. The 5,000 fervently French inhabitants of English Nova Scotia—the Acadians—would be removed and resettled, insuring English security on that vital peninsula. Finally a British fleet under Admiral Edward Boscawen would attack and drive away the French ships stationed in the St. Lawrence.

Limited warfare led only to defeat. Braddock marched to disaster in the summer of 1755. Near Duquesne the general was killed, 976 of his 1,500 regulars and 1,200 militiamen were killed or wounded; his successor immediately retreated to "winter quarters" in Philadelphia—in August! On hearing of Braddock's defeat, Shirley halted. Johnson was repulsed before he got to Crown Point, but fought off a counter-attack and was acclaimed a hero. The French fleet went unscathed. Only the campaign against the Acadians was successful. (Longfellow's *Evangeline* began her sorrowful trek.) The defeat of Braddock and Johnson, the hesitation of Shirley and Boscawen, emboldened the French and their Indians and from New York to the Carolinas the backcountry was bathed in blood and lighted with burning farmhouses.

Limited war became major war—America's "French and Indian War" and Europe's Seven Year War—in 1756 when England allied with Prussia against France and Austria. For England one disaster succeeded another until William Pitt rose to power. Egotistic ("I believe that I can save this nation and that no one else can") but able, Pitt realized as none had before that war in Europe was only part of a world-wide war. Subsidizing Prussia and leaving her to fight in Europe, he sent England's ships and men to India, the Caribbean, and America. The price was high— England's national debt almost doubled during the war—

but the French empire crumbled. In America in 1758 Louisbourg fell to General Jeffrey Amherst and Fort Duquesne to General John Forbes, although a third campaign —against Crown Point—ended in defeat when a combined British-American force commanded by General James Abercromby was ambushed by the French Marquis de Montcalm at Fort Ticonderoga just south of Crown Point. The next year Sir William Johnson (knighted after his 1755 Crown Point campaign) took Fort Niagara, General Amherst took Crown Point and cleared Lake Champlain, while General James Wolfe entered the St. Lawrence, found his way up the steep cliffs guarding Quebec, and defeated Montcalm on the Plains of Abraham—a battle which claimed the lives of both commanders. Within a matter of days Quebec was in English hands. The next year Montreal, the last French bastion, fell. To Americans, the war was over, but in Europe, India, and the Caribbean it continued for three more years. The French islands in the Caribbean and outposts in India were seized. When Spain entered the war as an ally of France, she was crushingly defeated in the Philippines and Cuba. For England it was a clean sweep. France, after three-quarters of a century of war, was prostrate.

The Treaty of Paris did not reflect this stunning victory, however. At the height of the war (1760) George II died and was succeeded by his son George III. The first two Georges had been content to leave the governance of England to the great lords of state who dominated Parliament. Young George was not. He intended the phrase "the King's government" to be taken quite literally—*his* government, not that of Walpoles or Pelhams or Pitts. Pitt must go, therefore, and in 1761 George obtained his resignation and elevated the Scottish Earl of Bute, a man who owed his position to the favor of the king rather than to influence in Parliament, to first place in the government. Bute, as Pitt would not have been, was outmaneuvered during the peace negotiations which culminated at Paris. In an amazing performance, France sold Britain peace rather than accepting a peace which all-conquering Britain could have dictated. True, Britain took all of North America east of the Mississippi—Canada from France and Florida from Spain—and territories elsewhere in the world. But Britain returned to France the rich Caribbean sugar islands of Martinique and Guadeloupe and fishing stations in the St. Lawrence, and to Spain the Philippines and Cuba. And Britain allowed the transfer of French America west of the Mississippi, including New Orleans, to Spain as compensation by France of her ally's losses. Having spent seventy million pounds on the war, one contemporary wrote, Britain paid the equivalent of thirty-four million for peace by relinquishing conquests.

In America, war's end, the "glorious peace"—for so Americans saw it—set off an orgy of patriotic sentiment. Britannia ruled and Americans were Britons. Statues were raised to Pitt and George III, the most popular of all English sovereigns. Yet even as men celebrated, small cracks in the empire were widening. A scant twenty years separated the first Treaty of Paris from the second by which Great Britain acknowledged American independence.

The Legacy of the Wars

In both Britain and America the wars—particularly those from 1739 to 1763—engendered attitudes dangerous to the peace and unity of the empire.

In America, British defeats such as those at Cartagena, Braddock's on the Monongahela, and Abercromby's at Ticonderoga led men to doubt the efficacy of the British army, while victories by colonials such as Pepperrell's at Louisbourg and Johnson's stand in 1755 gave them an unbounded faith in the prowess of colonial arms. Braddock and Pepperrell, regular and colonial, were particularly remembered. The Boston *Gazette*, following Braddock's defeat, wrote of "the cowardice of the British troops," lamented that New Englanders had not been sent to the Ohio and the regulars used for garrison duty, and reminded its readers that at Louisbourg there had been

New England troops led by a New England general. "The whole transaction gave us Americans the first suspicion that our exalted ideas of the prowess of British regulars had not been well founded," Benjamin Franklin wrote. Not only the efficacy but the intention of Great Britain to defend the colonies was cast in doubt as England, in the exigencies of peace-making, surrendered conquests beneficial to the colonies. Thus as Louisbourg fell for the second time, Israel Williams of Hatfield, Massachusetts, wrote that while he hoped that it would be retained he fully expected the French to be left in possession, "notwithstanding all our acquisitions elsewhere, and with a political view to keep us dependent."

Contact with the British military raised colonial hackles, too. Impressment into the navy and forced enlistment into the army were not uncommon, and as one observer wrote, "to see a drunken man lugged through the streets on a soldier's back guarded by others . . . must certainly give a strange impression of the method of enlisting and certainly have an ill effect on an inflamed mob." Colonial and crown officers clashed over precedence. For long an order-in-council stipulated that the junior regular officer take precedence over the senior colonial officer, to the annoyance of militia colonels edged aside by regular lieutenants. The demands for provisions and quarters precipitated numerous wranglings as colonial legislatures zealously guarded their prerogative to vote taxes. That the commander-in-chief of the British army in North America should, on one occasion, threaten to send two regiments into Philadelphia to find their own quarters if the Pennsylvania assembly did not vote supplies was hardly calculated to inspire good will. One can sympathize with the military mind as it coped not only with superiors in London but a dozen carping American legislatures, but one must also recognize the hostility toward the military provoked in the legislative mind.

Such grievances and attitudes faded with victory. Having won, the empire was forgiven all. Yet once provoked, the attitudes formed a substratum of thought to be resuscitated when conditions required. The American experiences of war did not directly contribute to the impending quarrel between the colonies and the English mother. But once that quarrel was underway, the memories of war exacerbated it. And once independence was in the wind, memories would lead men to think more favorably of a break than they might have done otherwise, and to consider a break feasible. Colonial militiamen watching the awesome advance of British redcoats on Breed's Hill in 1775 could comfort themselves with the thought that similar redcoats had been defeated on the Monongahela and at Ticonderoga.

In Britain, however, attitudes precipitated by wartime experiences were leading directly toward a confrontation with the American colonies, and toward independence.

The influence of the Board of Trade, as we have seen, had waned early in the century; the point of view it represented—absolute colonial dependence on Britain—had not been officially pressed. But that point of view persisted, kept alive by crown governors who were regularly frustrated by what they considered the too-powerful colonial legislatures, by men in the customs service who noted with despair that the extent of colonial trade was not reflected in the revenue, by merchants and manufacturers who came to look upon the American colonies as the most important yet most truculent part of the empire. Suggestions to curb American "independency," to undercut the colonial legislatures by paying executive officials from English revenues or by raising a colonial revenue by act of Parliament, even suggestions to garrison the colonies, were not uncommon. Yet such suggestions were lonely cries in a wilderness of official indifference until 1748.

In that year the Board of Trade was roused from its moribund state by the appointment to its presidency of George Dunk, Earl of Halifax, a man of ambition and energy who set about making his office more than it had been during the previous decades. By 1752 he had considerably augmented the powers of the Board within the English governmental framework. To the power to investigate and recommend he added that of nominating all colonial officers; all official correspondence between England and the colonies was to pass through the Board; Halifax himself was to be present at the Council whenever colonial matters were to be discussed. His influence was felt both at home and abroad. He pushed the idea of a Parliamentary tax to support crown officers abroad, supported an attempt to establish an Anglican bishop in the colonies, encouraged empire officials to contemplate ways in which colonial governments could be remodeled to make them more susceptible to imperial control, and embarked on a concerted effort to make the royal instructions to the governors binding upon colonial legislatures. The outbreak of the French and Indian War in 1754 curbed the reviving imperial viewpoint that Halifax both led and represented. Colonial support was necessary in the conflict with France; one could not ask for support and at the same time insist on reforms repugnant to the colonies. Thus Governor George Clinton was advised to desist from a quarrel with the New York legislature over legislative control of salaries during "the present urgency of affairs"; the governor of Massachusetts was told that "at a proper time" the Massachusetts house would be required to abandon its practice of exercising various executive functions, but "in the present situation of things" it would not be advisable. "Peace, unanimity, and a good understanding" were necessary "in the present situation of affairs," the Privy Council wrote in 1756. Reform could wait.

If the Anglo-French conflict curbed the budding reform movement, it also set the stage for reform, or at least change. For the war of 1754-1763 particularly brought home as nothing had before the fundamental disunity of the empire. The very arguments between legislatures and military commanders which inspired distrust for the mili-

tary in the colonial mind augmented a distrust of the legislatures in the British mind. The very people for whose
benefit the war had begun—so British officials reasoned—
would rather argue legislative prerogatives than support
the war. Calls on colonial legislatures for supplies and
troops precipitated debate and little else. Even after Pitt
promised that Britain would reimburse all their expenses
(and almost one million pounds was actually returned to
the colonies) the bickering continued.

Moreover, the very people for whose benefit the war
had begun persisted in trading with the enemy, giving the
enemy needed supplies and, by driving prices of colonial
goods high, depriving the British military of adequate
provisions. It was not that the colonials were disloyal. Far
from that. They were the most loyal of subjects, but subject also to self-interest, and they were disunited. What
concern of a New Englander that war was being fought in
Pennsylvania, or of a Pennsylvanian, once the war in
Pennsylvania was over, that it was being continued in the
Caribbean? Thus as Braddock began his march, forty ships
from American ports were unloading cargoes at Louisbourg; as defeat followed defeat in 1757 and 1758,
colonial vessels, under pretext of effecting prisoner ex-
changes, were unloading cargoes at Quebec; when French
Canada fell, colonists sent their ships to the Dutch island
of St. Eustatius in the Caribbean and to Spanish Montecristi where they met French vessels and effected a trade.
In 1760 Pitt learned that 100 vessels flying the English
flag had been counted in Montecristi harbor alone. Such
illicit trade, he wrote, "principally, if not alone, enabled
[France] to sustain and protract" the war, and he ordered
colonial governors to "take every step, authorized by law,
to bring all such heinous offenders to the most exemplary
and condign punishment." Customs officers began an energetic campaign against offenders, using the time-honored writs of assistance. Such writs, however, ran in the
name of the king and died when the king died, to be
reissued automatically in the name of the new monarch.

Thus the writs died with George II in 1760 and the Boston merchants took advantage of their death to fight the reissuance in the hope of depriving the customs men of their best weapon. Attorney James Otis' impassioned plea that the writs ran counter to the fundamental liberties of the citizen embedded in the British constitution would be lauded by the new republic. ("Then and there the child independence was born," John Adams would write.) But it had its roots in a mere commercial maneuver.

The bickering and quarreling, the lack of cooperation, the trade with the enemy—all this brought forth new calls to reorder the empire, to reduce the colonies to their proper dependence upon the mother country. During the late 1750s and early 1760s a deluge of recommendations poured in upon the Board of Trade and other crown ministries and offices, recommendations for garrisoning the colonies in order "to retain the inhabitants of our ancient provinces in a state of constitutional dependence on Great Britain," for a Parliamentary tax (a stamp tax, perhaps) with which to support crown officers in the colonies, for a stringent enforcement of the navigation acts, for a "new modeling" of colonial governments. Rumors of such recommendations spread, at least in Massachusetts, and in Boston one morning in 1760 John Adams met his friend Jonathan Sewall who told him: "These Englishmen are going to play the devil with us. They will overturn everything. We must resist them and that by force." About the same time the Boston *Gazette* reported that there was a move to overthrow the town meeting because it was "popular and mobbish."

The Fabric of Empire Tears

Certainly as the war closed what has been described as the "imperial clique" was determined to reform the empire, to make *de facto* the centralized empire which existed *de jure* in English minds. Yet to make a direct connection between this determination and the enactments of the 1760s which precipitated colonial opposition and eventually independence would be far too simple.

For one thing, the revival of the Board of Trade, the focal point of the imperial clique, was inextricably connected with the personality of Halifax, and when Halifax left the presidency of the Board in 1761 it reverted more or less to the moribundity in which he had found it. For another, the nature of the British government—a sprawling maze of offices, commissions, and boards, in none of which American affairs were even partially centralized after Halifax's departure from the Board—made the development of a concerted American policy impossible. Compounding the institutional flaw was the constant coming and going of ministers, the rejuggling of offices as George III attempted to find a government amenable to being "His Majesty's government" and Parliamentary factions strove first for cohesion and subsequently for power. Ministers appeared, were presented with a variety of American problems and advice as to how to solve them, applied their own solutions, and left the scene to be replaced by other ministers who were presented with other problems (more often than not the results of the first minister's solutions), other advice, and who applied other solutions. The pressure for centralization emanating from the imperial clique—more, the insistence that the empire *was* properly centralized, that colonial governments *were* dependencies—was the backdrop against which this drama of confusion was played. Ministers knowing little or nothing about America applied solutions predicated on absolute colonial dependence and were surprised that the Americans objected.

There were a myriad of American problems before the ministry as the war with France came to a close. Florida, Canada, and the vast transmontane territory were under British military occupation. How were these regions to be permanently established? There was a general and unquestioned assumption in the government that, having conquered half a continent, England must secure the conquest by establishing a permanent garrison in America. Where were the troops to be stationed? How were they to be maintained? Again: Colonial governments had through-

out the eighteenth century issued paper money, forced to
it by a lack of specie. The colonial paper had depreciated
and British merchants were fearful that they would be
required to accept the depreciated currency as payment
of debts due them. They sought an extension of an earlier
act of Parliament (1751) barring paper money as legal ten-
der in New England. And there was pressure to firm up
the navigation acts.

The ministry attacked its problems piecemeal. In Parliament bills began their slow progress toward enactment: A
Currency Act (passed 1764) by which colonial governments were barred from issuing further paper as legal ten-
der and required to retire all outstanding paper; provisions
for the enumeration of further colonial products to be
shipped only to England, for the revitalization of the old
Plantations Duty Act, and for bolstering the system of admiralty courts—all of which would find their way into a
general revenue act in 1764. The question of organizing
the conquered American territories was referred in the
Spring of 1763 to the Board of Trade for recommendations. But even as the Board considered, the problem was
aggravated by renewed warfare in mid-America as abandoned Indian allies of France rose under the leadership of
Pontiac. In due time the Indians were pacified and the
Board produced its recommendations: Organize Canada,
East Florida, and West Florida into new colonies; distrib-
ute some of the conquered territory to already established
British colonies (Georgia, Newfoundland, Nova Scotia);
temporarily set aside all the rest westward of "the heads
or sources of any of the rivers which fall into the Atlantic
Ocean" as an Indian preserve to be entered only by li-
censed Indian traders. The Board's recommendations,
slightly amended, were speedily accepted and embodied
in a royal proclamation of October 7. Pontiac's rebellion
also resolved the problem of where to station the army.
There had been several suggestions, but in the end some
of the troopers were retained in conquered Cape Breton,
Quebec, and Florida, while most were required in fighting

with the Indians. Where to station the troops was but half the question, however. Their maintenance was the other half. £350,000 per year would have to be raised to support an anticipated 10,000 troops (the establishment, as it turned out, was a little over 7,000). And it was not only money for the army which was needed. The administration of Nova Scotia and Georgia had for long been underwritten by Parliamentary funds; the new governments of East and West Florida were to be supported from London as well. The four governments required £20,000 a year. Moreover, there was a regular customs deficit—more money was required to maintain the customs system than was collected. In all, almost one-half million pounds sterling per year was needed.

Finances were the overriding consideration in British political thinking. The national debt was, in eighteenth century terms, astronomical and taxes, particularly on the English landed gentlemen who dominated Parliament, commensurately burdensome. Parliament insisted on relief and the ministry had of necessity to pare expenses to the bone—an austerity program amenable to the new First Lord of the Treasury, George Grenville, a man who believed "a national saving of two inches of candle" worth more than all Pitt's conquests. Aghast in 1763 (as Pitt had been before him) that it required £7,600 a year in American customs salaries to collect a mere £1,900 in revenue, he immediately set in motion a Treasury investigation into the seeming inability to collect *all* the customs due. The investigation led to an order that Fall forbidding the usual practice of officers appointed to the colonial customs living in England and relying on the services of half-pay deputies in America, to a circular letter to all colonial governors commanding them to assist the customs officials, and to an act of Parliament increasing the authority of British naval vessels in dealing with suspected smugglers and granting the crews which captured smugglers one-half the value of the prize.

The Treasury investigation and its results boded ill for

the future. Grenville was clearly breaking with the past and thinking of the empire not in traditional mercantile terms but in terms of Britain's immediate financial problems, of the acts of trade and navigation and the customs not as merely regulating trade but as sources of revenue. When called upon to supply the funds necessary to the army, his thinking of the empire in terms of revenue led him inexorably toward disaster. He asked for and obtained an act to raise a revenue in His Majesty's American dominions "for defraying the expenses of defending, protecting, and securing the same"—the Revenue Act of 1764 (sometimes called the Sugar Act). A variety of duties were laid on goods carried into or from America; the prohibitive duty on foreign molasses and sugar carried into the continental colonies was reduced (for the effort was not to curb the trade but to collect a revenue from it); stringent enforcement provisions were enacted. Grenville realized, however, that even yet he did not have a sufficient revenue to meet American expenses, and to colonial agents in England he introduced the idea of a possible additional act, one establishing in America the stamp duties which had for long been a part of the English financial system.

No broad policy lay behind any of these enactments. Disparate figures in the British government supported the measures for their own reasons. Thus Grenville supported an army establishment in America (even though it posed severe financial problems and threatened his austerity program) merely because the War Office said it was necessary. An ardent empire-minded officer supported an army because it would provide a position of strength from which Britain could "keep [the colonies] in proper subjection to the mother country." "I have no idea that we want military establishments against the Indians," a correspondent to the Board of Trade wrote prior to Pontiac's rebellion:

And as we have now no enemy to the northward, I do not know that any forts or soldiers will be wanted. . . . Yet if Canada is to be made a military government and a place of arms, I suppose it will be proper to imitate the policy of the French; they have already marked the proper places for stationing of troops in order to awe the British colonies. The lines of forts so much talked of before the war will restrain the colonies at present as well as formerly. The pretences for this regulation, must be, the keeping of the Indians in subjection, and making of roads, in which last work the troops ought actually to be employed, that they may be kept disciplined, and hardy.

Again, to Grenville, the fact that a revenue was to be raised in America was merely a necessity; to a member of Parliament struggling with the high taxes assessed on his land it opened a vista of relieving England of a part of her expenses and himself of a part of his obligation; to a member of the Board of Trade it was an opening gambit in an extended effort to undercut colonial legislatures. To English manufacturers, the proclamation barring settlement west of the mountains was desirable in that it would preclude the colonists from retiring "far into the woods... where they would raise and manufacture everything for their own use, without consuming anything from Britain, or being the least benefit to that country." But to military men and those involved in Indian relations, the proclamation was necessary to pacify the Indians and avoid friction between Indians and white settlers. To English land speculators it was necessary in that it removed the granting of lands from colonial capitals to London. And to the more fervent of the imperial clique, the drawing of "a very straight line... on the back of the provinces," beyond which lay Indians "encouraged to support their own sovereignty," was part of a broad scheme: "Surrounded by an army, a navy, and by hostile tribes of Indians... it may be time (not to oppress or injure [the colonies] in any shape but) to exact a due obedience to the just and equitable regulations of a British Parliament."

In America, however, men were not privy to this diversity of motivation. Faced with the deluge of laws, orders, and proclamations of 1763 and 1764, faced particularly with the Revenue Act and the hint of a coming Stamp Act, colonial political leaders envisioned a monolithic English government intent on changing what the colonists considered the just and equitable imperial arrangement, intent particularly on emasculating the powers of their legislatures. Thus Boston's town meeting, in instructing its deputies to the Massachusetts lower house, complained that the Revenue Act was detrimental to its trade. "But what still heightens our apprehensions," the burghers wrote, "is that those unexpected proceedings may be preparatory to new taxations upon us."

This we apprehend annihilates our charter right to govern and tax ourselves. It strikes at our British privileges which, as we have never forfeited them, we hold in common with our fellow subjects who are natives of Britain. If taxes are laid upon us in any shape without ever having a legal representation where they are laid, are we not reduced from the character of free subjects to the miserable state of tributary slaves?

And far to the south in Virginia the same argument was put forth in a memorial to the crown: "With humble confidence ... [we] entreat your majesty will be graciously pleased to protect your people of this colony in their enjoyment of their ancient and inestimable right of being governed by such laws respecting their internal polity and taxation as are derived from their own consent."

Moved by what they considered a threat to the prerogatives of their lower legislative houses, the colonial political leaders took the first step toward revolution. In private letters, memorials to the king, ministers, and Parliament, and through their agents in London, the colonials protested what had been done and was about to be done. Their protests proved to no avail. In March 1765 a Stamp Act *was* passed, to become effective on November 1. After that date every newspaper, almanac, pamphlet and broadside, legal document, insurance policy, ship's clearance, and license, every deck of cards and set of dice, was required to bear an official and costly stamp; any persons

selling, issuing, or utilizing unstamped materials were subject to trial without jury in admiralty courts. A Quartering
Act passed about the same time required civil authorities
in the colonies to furnish barracks and supplies to British
troops on request. The colonials memorialized and protested again, and added violence, mob action against the
stamp distributors appointed from England. They resorted
to economic coercion—non-importation agreements by
which merchants agreed not to purchase English goods
until the Stamp Act was repealed. And they cooperated
with each other—the Stamp Act Congress representing
nine colonies petitioning for redress on behalf of all. Non-
importation was by far the most effective weapon, for as
British exports to America declined, British merchants
pressed Parliament for a repeal. Grenville's ministry had
fallen to the exigencies of British politics, but the new
ministry of Charles Watson-Wentworth, Marquis of Rock-
ingham, effected a repeal of the Stamp Act early in 1766.

The events of the mid-1760s created an irreparable tear
in the fabric of empire. Colonial suspicions had been
aroused, for some men cast the British enactments in the
context of that negative theory of politics which was so
much a part of the political climate of the eighteenth century: Corrupted by power, the great lords of state—the
king's ministers—had brought the liberties of Englishmen
at home near to extinction; now those same ministers and
the Parliament they dominated were conspiring against
the liberties of Englishmen abroad. A government debt to
be serviced, taxation, a standing army—all had a well-
established place in the lexicon of this political theory as
the means by which corrupt men of power waged their
interminable war on liberty. And the very interminable-
ness of that war between tyranny and liberty suggested
that, although liberty had been maintained in the first
encounter, a second encounter would not be long forthcoming.

Moreover, leaders had appeared, men like Patrick
Henry and Richard Henry Lee in Virginia, Charles Thom-

son in Philadelphia, and Sam Adams in Boston, who would carry such suspicions to the people. Violence had been resorted to. The bully boys who stormed stamp commissioner Andrew Oliver's house in Boston and cowed commissioners everywhere tended to take credit for repeal on themselves; toasting their own prowess in the taverns, they would be quick to turn to violence again as opportunity offered.

But above all, two assumptions, each vital to the political system of its holder, had collided.

The colonials' political leaders had, as we have seen, evolved the notion of an empire of self-regulating parts. They had accepted Parliament in England as the legislative body of the empire as a whole and made of their own little parliaments the legislatures of the parts. This division of sovereignty was to them a "given," a basic assumption. But while they had been acting upon it, they had never formally stipulated their assumption in clear, unequivocable language, never published it for crown and Parliament to read, never thrown it in England's face (so to speak) as a constitutional, natural, and God-given right. In 1764-1766 they began doing just that. The colonial view of the sovereignty within the parts of the empire of their legislatures required, however, that Parliament in Westminster be *limited* in power, that there be some point beyond which Parliament had no authority and their little parliaments all authority. Yet England's constitutional development over the centuries had been toward the doctrine of the absolute supremacy of Parliament, toward an *unlimited* Parliament. Crown, ministers, and members of Parliament had not thought of themselves as innovators when they turned to the colonies to raise a revenue in 1764, for the supremacy of Parliament was such that nothing was beyond its power. The attempt to raise a revenue in the colonies violated the vital assumption of the colonial political leaders—the supremacy in their local spheres of their little parliaments. The colonials' rebuttal to this violation, their insistence that Parliament could not act, in turn vi-

olated the vital assumption of English political leaders—
the absolute supremacy of Parliament. Two opposite principles were in open confrontation.

The years of argument and debate to 1776 revolved
around this confrontation of principle. Parliament, in re-
pealing the Stamp Act, clearly enunciated its fundamental
principle in the accompanying Declaratory Act:

Whereas several of the houses of representatives in his Majesty's
colonies and plantations in America, have of late, against law,
claimed to themselves, or to the general assemblies of the same,
the sole and exclusive right of imposing duties and taxes upon his
Majesty's subjects in the said colonies and plantations; and have,
in pursuance of such claims, passed certain votes, resolutions, and
orders derogatory to the legislative authority of Parliament, and
inconsistent with the dependency of the said colonies and plantations upon the crown of Great Britain: may it therefore please your
most excellent majesty that it may be declared; and be it declared
... that ... Parliament assembled, *had, hath, and of right ought
to have, full power and authority to make laws, and statutes of
sufficient force and validity to bind the colonies and people of
America.*

The colonials, for their part, were less direct. They had,
in resisting the Revenue and Stamp acts, asserted that
Parliament's authority was limited. But the exact nature of
that limitation was vague. What was Parliament's to do?
What was theirs? Pamphlet after pamphlet addressed itself to the question. The colonists frequently fumbled, as
when a few attempted to distinguish between internal and
external taxes, the former within their jurisdiction, the latter within Parliament's, or between taxation for revenue
and taxation for regulation of trade. It is noteworthy, however, that they never successfully delimited Parliamentary
authority, never clearly distinguished between the power
of the center and the power of the parts. On the contrary,
toward the end of the pre-revolution quarrel they simply
denied that Parliament had any power over them at all.
The problem of defining a federal system—for in reality

that was what they were trying to do in the early years—
was passed to the new nation they would produce.

To Independence

The story of the pre-revolutionary argument can be told
in terms of symbols. Abstract political principles had collided in the early 1760s. In the years from 1766 to 1776
abstract principles as to colonial self-regulation and Parliamentary supremacy were in continuous confrontation. But
in the colonies the confrontation revolved around a sequence of symbols. And as the sequence proceeded, as the
memory of one phase of the continuing confrontation reinforced the next, as colonial leaders sought to understand
the totality of what they were involved in, they more and
more fell back upon the dichotomy of tyranny naturally,
always, and everywhere at odds with liberty, of con-
spiratorial men of power in England grasping for more
power by attacking liberty in America and themselves
necessarily resisting conspiracy, not only for their own
sake but for the sake of all humanity. What was merely a
suspicion in the early '60s became a certainty by the '70s:
a "conspiracy . . . first regularly formed, and begun to be
executed in 1763 or 4" existed; a "deliberate, systematical
plan of reducing us to slavery," Thomas Jefferson wrote;
"repeated, multiplied oppressions" had placed it beyond
all doubt "that their rulers had formed settled plans to
deprive them of their liberties."

The hated stamp symbolized the confrontation in 1765,
and the disappearance of the symbol with the repeal of
the Stamp Act saw an immediate abatement of controversy, despite the fact of the Declaratory Act, Quartering
Act, and Revenue Act (which had been amended but still
remained as a revenue-raising measure). When a new ministry in London, motivated by the same financial problems
which had directed the Grenville ministry plus the antipa-
thy of Parliament toward colonies which had denied its
supremacy, sent forth a new set of acts in 1767—the
Townshend Acts—the universal symbolism of the stamp

was absent and the colonial reaction consequently slug-
gish.

One of the new acts, named for Charles Townshend,
Chancellor of the Exchequer, punished the colony of New
York for its refusal to provide housing and provisions for
troops within the province as required by the Quartering
Act by declaring void all acts of its legislature until such
time as the law was complied with. Others established a
series of duties on goods imported into the colonies from
Britain—Townshend assuming that such "external" taxation would not bring any objection from Americans—and
effected reforms in the procedures for collecting the customs, establishing an autonomous American Board of Customs Commissioners separate from the English board.
Legislatures everywhere sympathized with New York but
did little and the Yorkers, fearful of standing "single in the
quarrel, and fall[ing] sacrifice to the indignation of the
commons of Great Britain," voted by a majority of one to
grant £1,500 for troop maintenance, although pretending
that the sum was a free gift to the crown rather than in
compliance with the Act, hence maintaining the colonial
principle of self-regulation. Efforts to combat the new duties by reactivating the non-importation agreements of the
Stamp Act days languished as merchants in each port held
back for fear of losing trade by acting before those of
other ports and agreements were not achieved on a continental scale until 1769. Only where the new customs commissioners were tangible symbols of the confrontation was
there a popular uproar akin to that of the stamp days.
When the uproar in Boston resulted in the dispatch of
troops to the town in 1768, the troops served as a symbol
for Boston and, to a lesser extent, all New England. And
when "baiting the lobsterbacks" led to the Boston "massacre" of 1770, the massacre became the symbol.

Not colonial actions but the unpopularity of the Townshend duties in England led to their repeal in 1770. The
duties, by taxing British goods, tended to discourage British exports to the colonies. They were, wrote one minister,

"so anti-commercial" that he wished they had never existed, "so preposterous" that he was amazed they had ever been passed by a British Parliament. Yet Parliament, too, proceeded in terms of symbols. In the face of colonial assertions the ministry was reluctant to withdraw the duties for fear of seeming to surrender to the colonial position until a new ministry, that of Frederick Lord North, proposed a solution: Repeal all the Townshend duties except that on tea; allow the tea duty, the preface to the Townshend Duty Act, and the Declaratory Act to stand as symbols of the confrontation. Americans accepted North's symbolism to the extent of ending non-importation on everything but tea.

Tea was uninspiring as a symbol, however, and quiescence seemed to return to America. Many, perhaps deluded by their own hope, thought the argument over, that North's partial repeal of the duties was a face-saving measure, and that in time all vestiges of Parliamentary pretense and the assault upon their liberty would be abandoned. But the more ardent colonial leaders were ever suspicious. They set about organizing and educating public opinion that it would be more attuned to an inevitable renewal of London's assault than it had been in '67. The specter of British military might was regularly set before the citizenry of Boston as March 5—Massacre Day—was celebrated with memorial services, bloody tableaux, and orations. A decision in London to pay certain public officials, including judges of the Massachusetts superior court, from England led in 1772 to the erection of "committees of correspondence" throughout Massachusetts, the committees "to state the rights of the colonists, and of this province in particular, as men, as Christians, and as subjects" and "to communicate and publish the same" together "with the infringements and violations thereof that have been, or from time to time may be made." The burning of the British revenue cutter *Gaspee* by Rhode Islanders and the establishment of a British "commission of inquiry" which seemed to remove the case from local

SYMBOLS OF EMPIRE AND REVOLUTION

George III In His Coronation Robes

Colonial Williamsburg Collection, Williamsburg, Virginia

Magna Britannia: Her Colonies Reduced
A political cartoon of 1768

Paul Revere's Engraving Of The Boston Massacre

THE ABLE DOCTOR, OR AMERICA SWALLOWING THE BITTER DRAUGHT, 1774

The able Doctor, or America Swallowing the Bitter Draught.

A SATIRICAL VIEW OF VIRTUAL REPRESENTATION, 1775

Courtesy of The New York Historical Society, New York City

jurisdiction led Virginians the next year to suggest a conti-
nent-wide system. The subsequent erection of committees
everywhere gave the Americans an inter-colonial organization independent of legally constituted governments
and a vehicle for transforming abstract considerations into
popular language which would soon be of use.

A colossal blunder on the part of Lord North set the
stage for overt revolution. The East India Company—Brit-

ain's arm of empire in southern Asia—was in financial
trouble and needed subsidization. Lord North, in mid-
1773, sponsored an act which in effect allowed the company a rebate of taxes other than the duty on tea shipped
to America and allowed it to erect an American monopoly
by sending tea directly from the east to its own distributors in America. (Previously the company had been required to ship its produce to England where it had been
sold to American wholesalers and transshipped to the
colonies.) Hopefully the company by virtue of shipping
directly to America, would be able to lower its prices and
increase its sales, hence its profits. Yet North had already
established tea as the symbol of the confrontation with
America; now, it seemed to Americans, he was attempting
to bribe them into swallowing their own principles and
destroying their own liberty with cheap tea—an interpretation which the committees of correspondence were
quick to place on the act.

Tea, heretofore a weak symbol, was suddenly a symbol
of the first magnitude and when the tea ships arrived a
wave of "tea parties" rocked the ports. Everywhere but at
Boston the tea was either sent back or stored away, tea
duty unpaid; in Boston, however, the royal governor insisted that the tea be landed and the duty paid. On the
night of December 16, therefore, 298 chests of tea valued
at 10,994 were thrown into Boston harbor. North and an
angry Parliament could not ignore the direct challenge of
the tea parties and, because of the destruction of property,
set out to make Boston and Massachusetts examples. By
act of Parliament (1774) the port was ordered closed until
the town made restitution for the tea. But this was only
the beginning. Companion acts set aside the Massachusetts charter and remodeled the government of the
colony: The power of the legislature was curtailed; the
colony's grand jury law and judicial system were revised;
the town meeting was limited. And the troops, which had
been withdrawn in the aftermath of the massacre, were

sent back into Boston, their commander, General Thomas Gage, being appointed governor of the colony. The series of acts was promptly dubbed "the intolerable acts" and momentarily symbolized the confrontation for the colonials. The continental denunciation of the intolerable acts; the arguments as local legislatures voted support of Massachusetts, fast days, and supplies for the town, and royal governors resisted; the meeting of a Continental Congress in Philadelphia in September and October of 1774 and the erection under the auspices of the Congress of a "continental association" to enforce non-importation, non-exportation, and non-consumption of British goods; the emergence of "committees of safety" in towns and counties all along the coast—all followed in close succession. In Massachusetts, minutemen began training. War materials were collected in strategic points around Boston. Finally the explosion of April 1775: General Gage sent a column to destroy military stores at Concord, precipitating a skirmish at Lexington and the rising of New England as minutemen assaulted the column on its return to Boston, then swarmed into the hills around the town, besieging the British garrison. To Americans, the physical invasion of a hostile army became a new symbol. It is you who are the "wicked rebel," John Cleaveland wrote to General Gage in the Essex *Gazette:* "A rebel against the authority of truth, law, equity, the English constitution of government, these colony states, and humanity itself."

What the colonists considered an effort to change the governance of the empire by depriving their little parliaments of the exclusive right to legislate in local affairs—an effort increasingly discerned as a conspiracy of tyrants against man's innate liberty—had led to open war. Through all of this, however, the colonists had remained loyal subjects of George III. Stamp distributors, customs commissioners, lobsterbacks, the intolerable acts—all symbolized a confrontation with Parliament and ministers, not king. Indeed, during the early years of argument, the king's governors were obeyed, even to the extent of the

Virginians going unrepresented in the Stamp Act Congress because their governor dissolved the House of Burgesses just as it was about to name representatives. As late as 1775 the same crowd which "huzzahed" for George Washington as he crossed Manhattan Island on his way to take command of the colonial forces around Boston rushed to the Battery to "huzzah" for a newly-arrived royal governor. Anglicans in the colonies prayed for the health of the king in conformity with the Book of Common Prayer, while in the taverns men drank the health of George and wished him the best of fortune.

This bumper I crown for our sovereign's health,
And this for Britannia's glory and wealth.

So went the last verse of "The Liberty Song," almost the national anthem of pre-independence days. Petitions and remonstrances directed to the king professed in all sincerity the loyalty of the colonists. And as the confrontation with Parliament and the king's ministers continued in time, as the colonists came to the position of denying Parliament any authority whatsoever over them, the king, to an ever increasing extent, symbolized the colonists' attachment to an empire which they had not yet considered leaving. "Allegiance to Parliament?" the Second Continental Congress asked rhetorically in 1775; "we never owed—we never owned it. Allegiance to our king? Our words have ever avowed it—our conduct has ever been consistent with it."

Allegiance could be stretched so far, however, before it would break. And colonial allegiance to king and empire was brought almost to the breaking point by Lexington and Concord. In New York and Georgia, militiamen seized control of the ports; in Williamsburg, militiamen (including students at William and Mary College) patrolled the streets to prevent the royal governor from seizing the arms in the public magazine. Extra-legal governments began making their appearance, in some cases extensions of the committees of correspondence, more usually the old lower houses of the legislatures sitting independently of the governor and council. Thus in Virginia, when the governor attempted to stop certain activities of the House of Burgesses by dissolving the House as had been done in Stamp Act days, the House, rather than meekly obeying him, trooped across the street to a tavern and went about its business, subsequently setting itself up as a supreme Virginia Convention. Soon after the governor fled to the safety of a British warship. By December 1775, royal governments had been swept away in all but New Jersey, although the proprietary governments of Pennsylvania and Maryland remained. By July 1776 these too were gone.

On an inter-colonial level, the Second Continental Congress met in May 1775 to remain in session throughout the remainder of the controversy and through the war years ahead. The delegates from the various colonies to the Congress immediately accepted the war situation which existed. In June an organization for war was created, the Congress assuming control of the forces besieging Boston and appointing Virginia's George Washington to command. To pay for the war effort, the Congress authorized the issuance of two million dollars in paper money. In July a "Declaration of the Reasons for Taking up Arms" was issued.

Yet war and independence were not synonymous, a fact which the members of the Congress pressed in their "Declaration." Their quarrel was still with corrupt ministers and a Parliament which had sought "all the easy emoluments of statutable plunder" by undertaking "to give and grant our money without our consent, though we have ever exercised an exclusive right to dispose of our own property." They were resisting only the "intemperate rage for unlimited domination" on the part of ministers and Parliament. This had led to war, but for their part military activities would cease "when hostilities shall cease on the part of the aggressors, and all danger of their being renewed shall be removed." They were not seeking to break with their "friends and fellow subjects in any part of the empire." "We assure them that we mean not to dissolve that union which has so long and so happily subsisted between us, and which we sincerely wish to see restored." In a petition to the king approved at the same time—the so-called "Olive Branch Petition"—their loyalty to George III was expressed in fervent terms, and that good monarch was humbly requested to intercede for them with Parliament and the ministry to obtain a repeal of the intolerable acts, the withdrawal of the troops, and a renunciation of Parliament's assertion of authority over the colonies. Some objected to what seemed a craven appeal. Massachusetts' John Adams, a delegate to the Congress, considered that the outbreak of war signified the end of such petitions and denounced the Olive Branch as putting "a silly cast on all our doings." But undoubtedly it represented the feelings of most of the colonial leaders. They were fighting to preserve their liberty within the empire as it had been prior to 1763 and as they had come to define it formally during the long controversy: Home rule under the king.

For over a year the Continental Congress remained in this anomalous position of leading a fight against the king's troops for liberty under the king. In July 1775, the Congress hinted at the possibility of looking for foreign aid against the king's army and shortly after set up a five-man "Committee of Secret Correspondence" for the purpose of corresponding with "friends in Great Britain, Ireland, and other parts of the world"—the last phrase ominously portending the future alliance with France. War supplies were purchased abroad and a navy provided under Commodore Esek Hopkins. To the north, Fort Ticonderoga was taken by "rebels" commanded by Ethan Allen and Benedict Arnold; the Battle of Bunker Hill (more accurately Breed's Hill) was fought June 17, 1775 and the siege of Boston went on; an unsuccessful march on Canada was set underway. All in the name of the king.

But the king would not accept the role assigned him by the colonists. He would not be their father and protector. Firm in his support of Parliament and his ministers, he curtly rejected the Olive Branch Petition in August 1775. Subsequently he proclaimed that the Americans were in a state of rebellion to his person.

In the situation the position of the colonists was somewhat unique and certainly difficult. The king was the only link to England and empire which they were prepared by this time to admit, yet the king refused to serve as such a link. As a consequence this last link had to be severed.

It was not easy to do. The colonial leaders were Englishmen. Their professions of loyalty to the monarch were and had always been sincere. If they discerned—and wrote of —a conspiracy to tyrannize in London, the king was no part of it, only his ministers and the Parliament they dominated. Moreover, the king over the years of argument had always been well presented. There was, in effect, little if any animosity toward him.

Still, the last link was severed. Gradually the person of the king began losing some of the sanctity attached to him. The action of the monarch in bluntly and personally refusing the Olive Branch tarnished his reputation, as did the hiring of German mercenary soldiers for the war in America. The various actions of royal officials "in the name of the king" rubbed off on the monarch—Falmouth, Maine, shelled; Norfolk, Virginia, shelled and burned. Then, in January 1776, an outright attack on the king appeared, the first of importance since the start of the troubles. This was *Common Sense*, a little pamphlet by Thomas Paine, an English radical newly arrived in Philadelphia.

Here the very institution of monarchy was attacked, and the English monarchy in particular:

Government by kings was first introduced into the world by the heathens, from whom the children of Israel copied the custom. It was the most prosperous invention the devil ever set on foot for the promotion of idolatry. The heathens paid divine honors to their deceased kings, and the Christian world has improved on the plan by doing the same to their living ones. How impious is the title of sacred majesty applied to a worm, who in the midst of his splendor is crumbling into dust!

England since the conquest hath known some few good monarchs but groaned beneath a much larger number of bad ones; yet no man in his senses can say that their claim under William the Conqueror is a very honorable one. A French bastard landing with an armed banditti and establishing himself king of England against the consent of the natives is in plain terms a very paltry rascally original. It certainly hath no divinity in it.

In England a king hath little more to do than to make war and give away places, which in plain terms is to impoverish the nation and set it together by the ears. A pretty business indeed for a man to be allowed eight hundred thousand sterling a year for and worshipped into the bargain! Of more worth is one honest man to society, and in the sight of God, than all the crowned ruffians that ever lived.

But the king, you'll say, has a negative in England; the people there can make no laws without his consent. In point of right and good order, it is something very ridiculous that a youth of twenty-one (which hath often happened) shall say to several millions of people older and wiser than himself, 'I forbid this or that act of yours to be law.'

George III himself was castigated as "the royal brute." Aristocracy was castigated for its continual exploitation of the people for the support of luxuries. All the difficulties of the last years were laid not merely to Parliament or the ministers, but to the king as the very leader of their conspiracy against liberty and the thought of reconciliation under the king was dismissed as ridiculous. Independence and a republican government were, to Paine, the common sense solution to the preservation of liberty in America. Sold in record numbers, passed from hand to hand and from tavern to tavern, the pamphlet was vital in creating a tyrant of George III.

The idea of a complete break with England spread. In April 1776, following the defeat of a group of loyalists at Moore's Creek Bridge in North Carolina, the provisional congress of that colony voted to instruct its delegates at the Congress in Philadelphia to vote for independence. At about the same time, a Massachusetts man was writing Sam Adams at Philadelphia: "The people are now ahead of you, and the only way to prevent discord and disunion is to strike while the iron is hot. The people's blood is too hot to admit of delays." John Adams confirmed this groundswell: "Every post and every day rolls in upon us, independence like a torrent." In Virginia the depredations of the British, including a threat to arm the slaves, roused feelings to a boiling point and on May 15 the Virginia Convention voted to instruct its Congressional delegates to introduce a motion for independence.

Congress, meanwhile, was acting for all the world like the congress of a sovereign and independent state. On March 14 the loyalists were ordered disarmed. On March 23 privateers were authorized. In April, American ports were opened to all foreign ships. In May, the Congress advised the individual colonies to reject any last remnant of British authority and establish governments which "in the opinion of the representatives of the people" would be most conducive "to the happiness and safety" of America. It was in the aura of this last, on June 7, that Richard Henry Lee, conforming to the vote of the Virginia Convention, rose in the Congress to move for the issuance of a declaration of independence, the formal solicitation of foreign alliances, and the establishment of an American federation. A bit of the old adherence to king and empire remained, however—a fear of independence and a hope that reconciliation might still be possible—and a formal vote on Lee's resolution was delayed. But a committee was appointed to draw up a declaration: Thomas Jefferson (then one of Patrick Henry's young lieutenants from Virginia), Benjamin Franklin, Roger Sherman of Connecticut, Robert Livingston of New York, and John Adams of Massachusetts. On July 1 Richard Henry Lee's original motion was voted upon and passed with the delegations of nine colonies assenting (exactly the number needed); on July 2 the remaining four delegations joined the majority; on July 4 the committee's draft declaration was read, amended, and adopted; on August 2 it was signed.

The Declaration was actually two documents combined in one. On the one hand, there was the very philosophical preamble, its second paragraph reading:

We hold these truths to be self-evident: that all men are created equal; that they are endowed by their Creator with certain unalienable rights; that among these are life, liberty, and the pursuit of happiness. That, to secure these rights, governments are instituted among men, deriving their just powers from the consent of the governed. That, whenever any form of government becomes destructive of these ends, it is the right of the people to alter or abolish it and to institute new government.

On the other, there was the great bulk of the document—the list or catalog of oppressive measures, the "repeated injuries and usurpations" of "the present king of Great Britain." The preamble asserted the propriety of revolution in terms of that eighteenth century political philosophy which we have referred to as Lockean. The second part of the Declaration—the catalog of evils done by the king—satisfied the logic of the colonial position as it had developed during the preceding decade: Having come to the conclusion that only the common king linked the colonies to England, the colonial leaders had logically to declare their independence from the king, and to justify the severance of their allegiance they had to associate George with all the evils and transgressions which they had been imputing to Parliament and the king's ministers. A few of the evils done to them by governors acting in the king's name the colonials could impute directly to the king: "He has refused his assent to laws, the most wholesome and necessary for the public good"; "he has dissolved representative houses repeatedly, for opposing with manly firmness his invasions of the rights of the people." But the crucial accusation was that "he had combined with others [his ministers] to subject us to a jurisdiction [Parliament's] foreign to our constitution . . . giving his assent to their acts of pretended legislation." With that George could be joined to what the colonials discerned as the conspiracy against their liberty and be accused of

. . . quartering large bodies of armed troops among us . . . imposing taxes on us without our consent . . . depriving us, in many cases, of the benefits of trial by jury . . . taking away our charters, abolishing our most valuable laws, and altering fundamentally the forms of our governments . . . suspending our own legislatures . . .

Of course, not all of the colonists went along with the Declaration, nor would all support the war that made it effective. John Adams, some time after the end of the war, described one-third of the colonists as having been "Patriot," one-third loyalist, and one-third neutral. There is a question about the accuracy of equal thirds, yet assuming that Adams was roughly right, how did this state of affairs come about?

First, we must recognize the fact that when, in the early 1760s, the quarrel began nearly all the colonial political leaders were aghast at what they conceived of as a Parliamentary and ministerial attempt to change the way of the empire in general and the rights and privileges of their assemblies in particular. Only a very few were committed to an imperial point of view and willing to place themselves and their colonies in a subordinate position in the empire. Very largely this group of original loyalists were persons, usually of large estate and standing in the colony, who had received royal offices—the Hutchinsons and Olivers of Massachusetts, for example. The generality, for the most part, put their trust in the political leadership and joined wholeheartedly in condemning the laws and orders emanating from England as an assault upon American liberty. The question to be decided by the individual was not whether or not to accept the changes being made, but what means should be used to resist. In 1763 and 1764 the method was petition and remonstrance, and nearly all could go along. In 1765 violence broke out. The individual was called upon to make a new decision: Are British actions of such magnitude as to require violence? Some, like Sam Adams, made the decision easily: Yes! These were the "Whigs." Others said no—the "Tories." Still others could not make up their minds and were neutral.

Over the years of continuing quarrel, as the measures of the ministry and Parliament became more blatant and the measures of resistance took on more and more an extra-legal aspect, people were constantly called upon to weigh (or reweigh) British measures against methods of resistance. Events such as the Townshend Acts, the Boston Massacre, the Intolerable Acts, Lexington, George's spurning of the Olive Branch—the overt British acts—threw many to the Whig side. The forming of a non-importation agreement, a committee of correspondence, a continental congress, a committee of safety, the outbreak of riot—the extra-legal acts of the Whigs—threw many to the Tory side. In 1776 the major question was posed: Do British actions over the years justify our separating ourselves from the empire completely and declaring our independence? A part of the populace answered in the negative and took action against the Revolution. From among these came the members of the various Tory legions raised for the British army, the bitterest of the crown's troops—bitter because for them at least this was a civil war, a war of brothers. Others answered negatively but remained quiet, passive supporters of the crown. Where the British army was long in occupation, as in Boston or New York, such Tories overtly cooperated and consequently emigrated when the troopers left, going to England or settling in Nova Scotia and upper Canada. Still others were so torn in their loyalties that they could not answer at all. But for that part of the populace answering positively, the Declaration cleared the air. American liberty could be preserved only by American independence. And the threat to liberty was personified in a single tyrant, albeit one manufactured during the months between *Common Sense* and the Declaration—George III. In a wild spree the populace set out to tear his statues down in New York and elsewhere, to tear down too all the symbols of royal authority, the coats-of-arms and royal unicorns on public buildings, much as the Protestants in the Reformation had torn down the symbols of Rome. George, once the toast and hope of empire, became the final symbol of the confrontation with England and was well on his way to that peculiar niche in history where Americans store their villains.

The War for Independence

Independence declared was not independence won. A war had to be fought.

Eighteenth century warfare was "rule book" warfare. Armies were small, highly trained in the art of march and countermarch, wheel and turn, for parade ground excellence was a necessary prerequisite to success on the battlefield where the basic weapon of the moment—the smooth bore, short range musket—dictated field tactics of advance in line, fire by volley, and charge with bayonet, the whole object being to break the enemy line before he broke yours. Generals looked upon battles as elaborate exercises in envelopment, counter-envelopment, double-envelopment. Princes, kings, and emperors looked upon war as a game of chess between rulers and on their armies, cities, and strongpoints as so many chessmen. Drive the enemy armies from this section of the board and it became yours; defeat his armies, seize his cities and strongpoints, take the enemy capital, and eventually, without waiting for annihilation, the opponent capitulates—indeed there is no annihilation in chess, only checkmate! And the players were expected constantly to cast up gains and losses, to be willing to negotiate from strong or weak positions, to buy or sell peace as the situation seemed to warrant. In such warfare, the citizenry counted for little.

The rule-book nature of eighteenth century land warfare explains much about the course of the War for American Independence. There was sporadic fighting in the west where the British, like the French before them, turned the Indians loose upon the frontier and American frontiersmen sought to pick off the British forts. On the seas American privateersmen and naval officers such as John Paul Jones fought glorious (and sometimes inglorious) single ship actions. But American independence was decided in a series of campaigns in the coastal areas of the settled colonies, and here the British fought by the rules.

To an extent, so too did the Americans. The Continental Congress thought and voted in terms of a small army fighting a limited war of maneuver. Thus the famed "continentals" of Washington's army were organized and trained along European lines, first at Boston where Washington enlisted 10,000 men in continental service and later by European volunteers such as the Baron von Steuben who wrote the army's drill manual—the "blue book" which became the military bible of the continentals. The Americans' rule-book army, however, was little more than a veneer. Beneath it was a mass army of militiamen, ordinary citizens who, with little training or equipment, occasionally fought British columns guerilla-style but more often rose up to join the regulars for brief periods, giving a weight of numbers if nothing else. And the rule-book army masked the fact that American leaders were not fighting by the rules when it came to war or peace, that the Congress was actually fighting a war of annihilation on behalf of the people, having in the Declaration mutually pledged "our lives, our fortunes, and our sacred honor" to the cause of annihilating the imperial connection. Actually the best service that the American army did was to maintain its own existence—a difficult task, for enlistments were too often short-term and desertion common—and thereby direct British military might against itself. It gave the British something to fight and defeat during the first stage of the war and something to watch during the second. British military commanders were able to envision the war in rule-book terms (as they could not if the Americans had fought as a patchwork of partisan bands) and fight and lose it according to the rules.

The first phase of the war was one of British assault. Outmaneuvered by the Americans who placed the guns captured at Ticonderoga on Dorchester Heights commanding Boston harbor, the British in March 1776 cut their losses by abandoning the town. Major General Sir William Howe assumed command from Gage, regrouped and received reinforcements in Nova Scotia, and with 400 transports, 30 warships, and 32,000 men struck at New York, defeating Washington's army at the battle of Long Island (August 1776). In the best European fashion, Howe offered terms in the aftermath of victory and when his terms were refused pressed on. Newport, Rhode Island, was taken by a seaborne expedition. Washington was edged off Manhattan, defeated at White Plains, and chased across New Jersey and into Pennsylvania (September-December 1776), although a winter sally into New Jersey revitalized his dispirited army.

In 1777 the British again pressed the offensive. Howe thrust toward Philadelphia, the American capital, outmaneuvering and defeating Washington at Brandywine Creek, taking the city, and defeating Washington's counterthrust at Germantown (September-October). From Canada, a British army under General John Burgoyne marched south along the old invasion path (Richelieu River, Lake Champlain, Lake George, the Hudson River) intending to cut New England from the remaining colonies. Howe's capture of Philadelphia—a signal for capitulation in the rule book—signalled nothing; the Congress merely took itself elsewhere. Burgoyne's force, while an easy match for the few regulars opposing him, was no match at all for the thousands and thousands of militiamen who rose to block his path. The militiamen compacted his army by nipping off one foraging column (at Bennington, Vermont) and thus dissuading him from sending out others; they afforded a mass reserve as the regulars skir-

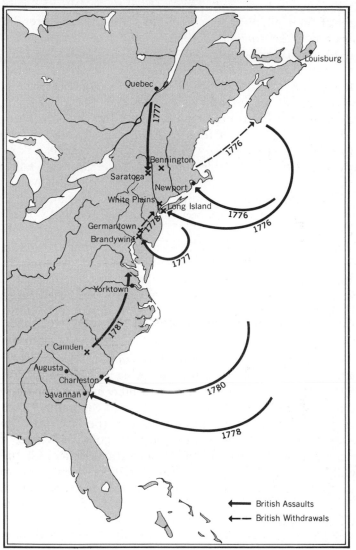

Louisburg

Quebec

1777

Bennington

Saratoga

Newport

White Plains

Long Island

1776

1776

1776

Germantown

1777

Brandywine

1778

Yorktown

1781

Camden

Augusta

Charleston

1780

Savannah

1778

→ British Assaults
⟶ British Withdrawals

mished with Burgoyne's redcoats and German mercenaries at Freeman's Farm and Bemis Heights; and by the very fact of their numbers they brought Burgoyne to surrender his army at Saratoga on October 17. For the British, defeat (at Saratoga) and victory (at Philadelphia) balanced each other and signified the possibility of a negotiated peace. Hence they offered the Americans favorable terms which, however, did not include independence. For a European adversary the terms might well have offered a way out of a difficult war, but not for the Americans. Indeed, in the aftermath of Saratoga they found an ally in France. Taking advantage of the troubles her old adversary had fallen into, France accepted the proferred hand of the Americans, signed treaties of amity, commerce, and alliance in February 1778, and entered the war. Subsequently France's old ally Spain joined the contest, although, more cautious than France, she declined an alliance with rebellion. The war went on, a world war now, as the old wars for empire had been. In America, however, the frustrated British commanders in a sense gave up. They had taken the strongpoints, even the capital, and defeated the army. What more could they do to win?

In 1778, Major General Sir Henry Clinton having replaced Howe, the British command could think of nothing better to do than abandon Philadelphia and return to New York, Washington trailing along to take up a waiting station at White Plains. The second stage of the military confrontation began as, grasping at straws, the British began a series of adventures in the Southern colonies where, it was thought, loyalism would throw the balance, all the while holding the bulk of their forces in New York to watch the watching Washington. In December, Savannah, Georgia was taken by a small expeditionary force; Augusta fell and royal government was re-erected in the colony. A year later, an American-French assault on Savannah having been beaten off, Clinton was emboldened to bring 8,000 troopers south. Charleston was invested and surrendered in May 1780. British garrisons were sprinkled about

South Carolina and the province was considered pacified when Clinton returned to New York, leaving General Lord Charles Cornwallis in command. Congress sent General Horatio Gates, the commander but not hero at Saratoga, into the South, but Gates' few regulars and militiamen were ripped apart at Camden (August 15-16). Thereafter, however, Cornwallis' excursions northwest toward North Carolina were met by the same combination of regulars (now under the command of General Nathanael Greene) and irregular militiamen which had stopped Burgoyne, and the British could gain nothing better than half-victories.

Meanwhile a small British force had raided into Virginia. Cornwallis, in the Spring of 1781, moved north to assist (while the American Greene moved south to pick off the British garrisons in South Carolina). Cornwallis could not even bring the small force of continentals in Virginia to battle, however, the American commander, the Marquis de Lafayette, leading him a "country dance" which ended only with the British retiring to the sea at Yorktown. Succor from a British fleet was denied Cornwallis when a French fleet, momentarily cooperating with the Americans, turned the British ships away in a battle off the Chesapeake Capes. Washington, with 5,700 continentals from New York and a French army of 7,000 joined Lafayette to bring about Cornwallis' surrender October 19, 1781 in a classic eighteenth-century siege operation.

The British in the first stage of the war had failed to win despite the rule book. But the same rule book said they had not lost. The capitulation of Cornwallis was something else again. Within their rules it could, if they chose, be the decisive event. They so chose. "Oh, God! It is all over," said Lord North when he learned of Yorktown. In March 1782, Parliament admitted it was over by voting to "consider as enemies to his Majesty and the country all those who should advise or by any means attempt to further prosecution of offensive war on the continent of North America." Peace negotiations were opened with American commissioners in Paris and, on November 30, 1782, preliminaries were agreed upon. On the anniversary of Lexington, April 19, 1783, Congress ratified the treaty which was signed at Paris in September. Independence was recognized and the new nation given generous boundaries—westward to the Mississippi, southward to Florida (which Britain returned to Spain) and north to Canada and the Great Lakes. That Fall British troops left their bastions to sail for home. As the last of them left New York on November 25, Washington's continentals marched down from White Plains and into the city, keeping step with a nonsense ditty:

> *Doodle, doodle, doodle dandy,*
> *Corn shocks, rum, and a homemade brandy,*
> *Indian puddin' and a pumpkin pie,*
> *And that'll make the Yankees fly.*
>
> *And every Yankee shall have on his back*
> *A great big pumpkin in his sack,*
> *A little molasses, and a piece of pork,*
> *And away we'll march straight for New York.*

The ditty was British in origin, having been sung by red-coats on their earlier march from Philadelphia to New York. Its tone then had been one of derision. But the Americans adopted the derision as a badge of honor, and sang it proudly.

8.

Revolution and Nation

IN THE CAULDRON of revolution
the American leaders' perception of themselves was odd
indeed. They were rebels and a traitor's death conceivably awaited failure. And while their rebellion was the result of felt injuries, once independence had been declared
they thought little of that long catalog of sins committed
by the king which they had appended to the Declaration.
Rather than rebels concerned with the past, they perceived themselves to be dedicated servants of a bright
future for all mankind.

Their attitude is not inexplicable if we keep in mind the
eighteenth century political thought which they carried
into the Revolution and by which they perceived the
events in which they were involved. Increasingly through
the years of imperial conflict they saw the argument with
Britain in terms of the never-ending war between tyranny
and liberty. They cast Parliamentary leaders, king's ministers, finally George III himself, in the roles of corrupt men
made more corrupt by power and seeking to tyrannize all
men; and increasingly they saw themselves in the role of
liberty's heroes fighting mankind's battle against tyranny.
The tyrannizing forces in England being implacable, they

had, as they saw it, been forced to independence. In good Lockean fashion, they had withdrawn their consent from the governmental system. They were, consequently, reduced to their natural liberties. But because men cannot exist in a natural state, they had to write new compacts—explicit compacts, hence their concern for written constitutions, rather than the implicit compact of theory—establishing new governments not only for themselves but "for millions yet unborn," a phrase that rings in the oratory and literature of the period.

The task confronting America's leaders was, to them, invigorating and exciting. "You and I, my dear friend," John Adams wrote in 1776, "have been sent into life at a time when the greatest lawgivers of antiquity would have wished to live. How few of the human race have enjoyed an opportunity of making an election of government for themselves or their children." Yet it imposed, in their minds, a heavy responsibility, for to erect a bad governmental system would make a mockery of their destruction of the old: "Should a bad government be instituted for us in the future, it had been as well to have accepted . . . the bad one offered to us from beyond the water," Thomas Jefferson wrote. It imposed, too, an enormous moral burden upon Americans. In the shadow of the failure of one government, they perforce concerned themselves with rectifying the causes of that failure. And inasmuch as the failure had been—in their negative philosophy of government—inherent in the corrupt nature of man which led any man of power to misuse power, they envisioned both a reform of the nature of man and the establishment of governments immune to man's corruption. Thus they would have republics, not simply because they would have no king, but because the very word implied to them the end for which governments were properly erected—*res publica,* the public good—and because republicanism allowed government to emerge from and be responsible to the people who constituted the public and could not, *en masse,* act contrary to their own good. And they would have people individually virtuous, sublimating themselves, their private goals, and their ambitions to the public weal. For the Americans knew—their reading of history taught them—that the greatest danger to republics was the individual running his own course without regard for the total society.

In all of this, the American leaders perceived of themselves as innovators. With their concern for the future, the audacious newness of what they were doing—erecting republics in a world of monarchies—they could hardly avoid it, and in the early 1780s they designed the Great Seal of the United States with its awesome motto: *Novus Ordo Seclorum*— "Towards a New Order of the Ages."

We cannot ignore this self-perception. It emboldened America's leadership. It was to be a fundamental facet of the national identity which emerged from the Revolution. Yet we cannot be swept away by the high level of political abstraction which marked the writings of the period from independence to the Constitution into thinking that here were, in reality, men who had stepped out of time, who did things without reference to what had gone before. We must remember, as one historian has pointed out, that 95 per cent of those who filled an office before the Revolution held public office in either state or federal government after the Revolution, and that self-perception was always tempered by experience.

A League of Sovereign Republics

Independence posed a paradoxical problem. On the one hand it was infeasible that the thirteen colonies—now conceivably thirteen sovereign states—should remain apart. With the Declaration of Independence they were inseparably joined in rebellion and the exigencies of war forced at least coordination upon them. But beyond that they had been, throughout their existence, united as parts of one British body politic, however loosely constructed colonial leaders considered that body to be. Colonial political leaders had felt their local institutions to be paramount in regard to local affairs, but left to London, as their common hub, the direction of inter-colonial affairs, commerce, foreign policy, and defense. Having broken with London, they needed something to replace London.

On the other hand, however, the American leadership was innately provincial. Dealing with the colonial world as a whole, we have tended to accentuate the similarities between colonies. But in that relatively immobile age, when a trip of 100 miles was more than the equivalent of a transatlantic jet flight, they themselves stressed their differences and were far more oriented to the particular governments of their colonies and states than to a central government—be it in London or one of their own fabrication.

Indeed, throughout the colonial period, all attempts at institutionalizing inter-colonial cooperation had failed in the face of this provincialism. The New England Confederation of the seventeenth century had provided for the regular meetings of commissioners from the member colonies and their joint action in emergencies. But Massachusetts Bay had, in effect, destroyed the Confederation when her sister members, in their own interests, attempted to make the decisions of the assembled commissioners binding. A congress called by London on the eve of the Anglo-French confrontation on the Ohio (1754) to consider measures for a common defense produced a "Plan of Union" which would have joined the colonies for certain limited purposes under a President-General appointed by the crown and a Grand Council of delegates elected by provincial assemblies. But generally ignored, the Albany Plan, in the few colonies where it was considered, was vehemently denounced as "subversive of the most valuable rights and liberties of the several colonies included in it, as a new civil government is thereby proposed to be established with great and extraordinary powers . . . inconsistent with the fundamental rights of these colonies . . . and destructive of our happy constitution." In the mid- and late-1770s, when the former colonials considered a central government, the same feelings prevailed, even exacerbated by the pre-revolutionary debate, for had not the central government in London (to their way of thinking) sought the destruction of the local autonomy which they cherished? Would not another central government be prone to do the same?

The problem of a necessary centralization versus a suspicion of centralization was resolved by compromise: Union on the basis of a central government so weak that it could never pretend to dominate the thirteen sovereignties banded together under it. In 1776, in response to Richard Henry Lee's motion in the Second Continental Congress for a declaration of independence *and* the establishment of an American federation, a committee was appointed to consider the latter. Subsequently it brought forth a plan which merely allocated to an American government the powers which the former colonials had been willing to entrust to London. Even such a union was considered too strong by the state delegates in Congress, while a stipulation in the plan that the union of the states was to be indivisible, that they were "never to be divided by any act whatever," simply would not do. Only after considerable amendment designed to weaken the central government still further was the draft plan adopted as the Articles of Confederation and sent to the state legislatures for their approval.

The Articles dispatched to the states for ratification in 1777 were not ratified by all (and hence not effective) until 1781, the result of a conflict over the possession of western lands by some states and their non-possession by others. Maryland, a have-not state, withheld its consent until first New York, then Virginia consented to relinquish western land claims to the Congress. As a consequence, the extra-legal Continental Congress directed the Revolutionary War. But this delay actually made little difference, for the Articles were nothing but a formal statement or definition of the congressional government already in existence. Limited powers of defense, coinage, and the conduct of foreign affairs were delegated to a unicameral congress consisting of delegates from each state, each state having a single vote in determining affairs. The Congress' law-making powers were limited to recommendations which might or might not be adopted by the states. It could not levy taxes, only requisition monies from the states. It had no power to regulate trade. There was no national judiciary, only a cumbersome arrangement for arbitrating disputes between states. There was no chief executive, only a "committee of states" and separate secretaries or commissions for foreign affairs, war, finances, post office, and admiralty appointed by and responsible to Congress. There were to be frequent hiatuses —there would be no secretary for finances through 1782 and 1783, for example. And "each state," to quote the Articles, was to retain "its sovereignty, freedom, and independence, and every power, jurisdiction, and right which is not expressly delegated" to Congress. The American Confederation was to be simply—again in the words of the Articles—"a firm league of friendship... for their common defense, the security of their liberties, and their mutual and general welfare."

If a prejudice against central government dictated the form of this "firm league of friendship," state constitutions were considered vital. The earliest ones were written in the hectic days of 1776 and 1777, in one case overnight in a tavern.

To their state constitutions, but not to the Articles, the political leaders prefixed an enunciation of their Lockean philosophy. In Pennsylvania's: "Whereas all government ought to be instituted and supported for the security and protection of the community as such, and to enable the individuals who compose it to enjoy their natural rights ... and whenever these great ends of government are not obtained, the people have a right by common consent to change it...." In Virginia's: "All men are by nature equally free and independent, and have certain inherent rights, of which, when they enter into a state of society, they cannot by any compact deprive or divest their posterity. . . . " To the state constitutions, but not to the Articles, they appended "bills of rights," lists, really, of the natural rights of the individual upon which government could not trespass. And generally in providing new governments for the states, the constitution writers merged theory with experience in a complex although not always consistent pattern.

Everywhere but in Connecticut and Rhode Island governments were in shambles. Royal and proprietary governors, councils, and officeholders had been swept away; lower legislative houses had become revolutionary and all-powerful bodies. In Connecticut and Rhode Island, where there had never been royal governments, the regular colonial governments were *in toto* revolutionary, and in the aftermath of independence their seventeenth century charters were merely declared "excellent constitutions of government"; with a few amendments tacked on, they were to continue in force until 1818 and 1842 respectively. Yet if the old governments were gone, the former colonials worked with the prime elements of government known from the colonial years —governor, council, and lower legislative house—collecting the debris of the old as the components of the new. And if they were guided by their new republicanism, they operated within the confines of an eighteenth century conception of government assumed from Britain: Power in government must be divided, else one man or group of men, unchecked, would tyrannize; the elements of government among which power was divided properly derived their authority from and represented the basic divisions of society—as in England the king represented himself, the House of Lords the aristocracy, and the House of Commons the people. Together the parts of government, as the parts of society, formed a balanced whole, no part of government nor division of society able to dominate another. By *people* one meant men of at least some property who, by virtue of that property, had a stake in an orderly society and hence properly a voice in society's affairs.

Out of their new republicanism, America's political leaders, in writing their new constitutions, accented that element of government which in eighteenth century theory represented the people—the lower legislative houses. Yet given the fact that they thought of the people in terms of the propertied, the suffrage was, as it had been in the colonial period, generally confined to the propertied; only in Pennsylvania and Georgia was the suffrage broadened, and in both states all adult, male taxpayers were allowed to vote. Out of their colonial past, the leaders revived the office of governor (with the exception of Pennsylvania where the governor's functions were given to an elected council of twelve). They revived, too, the legislative function of the colonial council, establishing in all but Pennsylvania and Georgia (which had unicameral legislatures before the Revolution) some form of "senate." But the powers of both governors and senates were held to a bare minimum. The distrust of governors and councils carried over from the colonial period and particularly the years of pre-independence quarreling when the governors and councils had seemed so willing to do the bidding of tyrannizing ministers in London.

The revival of governors and councils, even with minimal powers, left the American leaders with a question of theory: If each element of government represented a part of society, what parts did governors and councils represent? Their initial answer was that inasmuch as all men of property elected and were represented by the lower legislative houses, men of greater property should be represented by senates and governors. Hence they wrote into their constitutions ascending property qualifications for gubernatorial and senate offices. But such an answer did not satisfy. It posed still other questions. If the parts of their new governments represented the parts of their societies, should not the parts be equally balanced and governors and senates have power enough to balance the representatives of the people? And if such a balancing was effected to the denigration of the people's power, would not the government cease to be a republic? In the decade following the first state constitutions such questions were furiously debated in the states. And gradually Americans abandoned the eighteenth century's idea of governments representative of society's parts, effecting, as historian Gordon S. Wood has written, a revolution in political thought. *All* elements of government properly derived their authority from and represented *all* the people; the balance to be sought—that balance of power between parts which would preclude tyranny—was not properly between parts representative of the parts of society but between parts differentiated only by their functions in government: executive, legislative, and judicial. The new concept underlay new state constitutions, for indeed most of the early ones were soon rewritten and governors and upper houses left weak in the first constitutions were strengthened in the later so as to effect the balance. And it would underlie the Federal Constitution of 1787.

The Fledgling Nation

In practice the state governments that were created in 1776 and 1777 were junior partners to the Continental Congress during the war. They supplied money, provisions, and troops to the Congress, even maintained navies and armies of their own, but the Congress led. As war ended, however, the Congress became junior to the states in reality as well as in intent. In the hectic days following peace, riots broke out among disbanding troops in Philadelphia; the riots forced Congress to leave the city and wander—to Princeton, Annapolis, Trenton, finally New York—talking incessantly about where to set themselves permanently, a matter of as little consequence to one Connecticut leader as was the Congress itself. The delegates elected by the state legislatures were too often second-rate men, and the delegates in turn were too often absent. During the first four months of 1784, for example, the

Congress had a quorum on hand (at least two delegates from each of nine states) for only three days. This decay of Congressional leadership was natural, for the problems of the moment were internal problems and Congress was not expected to concern itself with affairs within the states.

The internal problems were myriad, most emanating from the economic chaos which followed the war. Hard-fought campaigns in lower New York, Virginia, and the Carolinas had resulted in physical devastation, compounded in the Southern states by the loss of black slaves carried away by the British army and the consequent diminution of the labor force—South Carolina alone lost approximately 25,000 slaves, Virginia approximately 30,000. State governments were deeply in debt, their treasuries empty; Virginia's Governor Benjamin Harrison dolefully reported that he had but four shillings on hand in 1782 and "no means of getting any more." The end of the war meant armies were no longer purchasers and consumers, and a post-war depression descended upon the continent.

The physical damage of war could easily have been repaired and the depression surmounted. Indeed, the very act of setting devastated areas aright tends to initiate the economic activity necessary to invigorate a lagging economy—a phenomenon familiar to the twentieth century. And America's one great asset, her soil, was untouched, the produce of the soil soon moving from farm and plantation to port to be sent overseas to the profit of the entire society. There was, however, the coexistent problem of reorienting the trade of the nation.

As colonies, the American states had been protected within a world-spanning British trading network. Farm produce entering the ports had flowed out along traditional routes to well-established markets, passing through merchants who utilized the financial facilities of London to keep tab of debits and credits. Independent, the former colonies found themselves thrust out of the parental home, so to speak, and forced to find their own way in the world. Traditional routes, established markets, and London's financial facilities were no longer invariably open to the Americans, for quite logically Mother Britain admitted her former children only to those trades which were beneficial to her own interest, giving no thought—as she had when they were within the empire—to their well-being. Thus British merchant houses were encouraged to return their factors to Virginia and Maryland and again purchase tobacco for consumption in Great Britain and resale throughout Europe. But New England and Middle states produce was barred from the British islands of the Caribbean. British manufacturers were allowed to export their goods to America as before, although in British flag vessels. The closing of the Caribbean islands, however, meant that the Northern states had no proper return to make for the imports they received—recall that prior to the Revolution New England and the Middle colonies had retained a roughly favorable balance of trade by paying for British imports with the receipts of their sale of agricultural produce in the British West Indies. Consequently they had to pay in specie for their British purchases on the basis of an unfavorable trade balance. Hard money drained from America, forcing seven of the states to resort to paper money, with depreciation a factor, particularly in Rhode Island. Moreover, Mother Britain would no longer buy ships from the New Englanders, preferring to foster her own shipbuilding industry. Massachusetts, which had annually built 125 vessels prior to the Revolution, half of them for sale to British merchants, launched but twenty-five a year in the 1780s. New England fishermen were barred from their time-honored practice of drying fish in Newfoundland and Labrador, foreign territory now. And of course Britain would no longer pay a bounty to South Carolinians to encourage the production of indigo, nor to North Carolinians to encourage naval stores production. Indigo exports dropped to next to nothing as a consequence—a British protective duty on rice aggravating the situation in South Carolina—while North Carolina's exports dropped two-thirds.

The states, individually, attempted to bolster their flagging economies. Virginia and Maryland opened their borders to British merchants in 1783. Patrick Henry's rhetoric, once so effective in arousing suspicions of the British, was applied to ending those suspicions when the repeal of Virginia's wartime laws calling for the seizure and condemnation of British goods was under debate: "Their king has acknowledged our independence—the quarrel is over—peace has returned." Tobacco flowed from the Chesapeake once again and recovery was swift, retarded only in the mid-1780s by the peculations of a Pennsylvania entrepreneur who, having contracted to supply the whole French nation with tobacco, utilized French money to force tobacco prices down.

Other states recovered more slowly. To the south, the Carolinas and Georgia opened a direct trade in rice to the European continent. The Northern states' provisions trade to the West Indies revived somewhat as the French islands admitted American ships and British island officials, their people in need of what the Americans had to offer, broke the spirit of British law by certifying as "under distress" the most seaworthy and fully laden American vessels, allowing the distressed vessels "shelter" and a chance to sell their cargoes. More important, however, merchants sought to enlarge an old trade to the Mediterranean and explored the possibilities for profit in areas where they had formerly been barred from trading, particularly in the Far East. Banks were established in Philadelphia, New York, and Boston to take the place of London as a source of commercial credit—there had been no banks in colonial America. And to a small extent there was a tendency to divert capital from commerce to manufacturing, continuing a trend which had begun when revolution and war cut the European trade of the colonies.

State governments encouraged such private activity, establishing mercantilistic customs and tonnage duties to protect their own ships, trade, and manufactures at the expense of others, even those of other states. They worked assiduously to stabilize state finances, applying customs duties, land, and poll taxes not only to state operating expenses but to state debts as well, even to the extent in certain states of assuming the debt owed by the Confederation Congress to the citizens of the state. (Public creditors were largely merchants and businessmen, hence the amortization and interest payments on state and national debts put capital in the hands of those who could use it to send ships to sea, or establish manufactories.) Yet not all states were equally capable of dealing with financial difficulties. Virginia, its trade reaching prewar levels early in the 1780s, managed its debt and amassed a surplus easily, as did New York. But Massachusetts' finances were stabilized on a sound basis only by putting an excessively heavy load on its property and poll-tax systems, eventually creating widespread discontent in the purely agricultural regions of the state. And states like New Jersey, Connecticut, and Delaware—without customs duties and entirely dependent upon internal resources—found fiscal recovery inordinately difficult.

In only one area was the Congress of the Confederation expected to assist the states in solving their internal problems, that of foreign policy. American merchants, sending their vessels into the Mediterranean in search of expanded trade, discovered the cruel fact of Mediterranean piracy, for their ships were no longer protected by either the British navy or the tribute paid by Great Britain to appease the Barbary states. The merchants looked to Congress for relief. Congress was expected, by maintaining consuls and agents abroad, to facilitate commerce and, by negotiating favorable treaties, to assist in opening new areas to American merchants. Above all, the merchants insisted that American diplomacy open the British West Indies to their trade.

Foreign policy is a matter of give and take, however. The Congress sought to take while having little to give in exchange. Even American friendship was not worth much, for in a world of diplomacy where friends were sought for the power they could exert, America was powerless. She had no army or navy to speak of. Her government—for to foreigners the Congress *was* the government—could not even offer trade advantages in America in exchange for trade advantages abroad, for each state regulated its own commerce.

Indeed, the Congress could not apparently preserve the territorial integrity of the nation as, in one area after the other, secession movements developed. The good citizens of Nantucket Island, their whaling fleet decimated by war and recovery blocked by a high British tariff on whale oil, petitioned the Massachusetts legislature to be allowed to secede so that they could re-ally themselves to Britain and "return to the benevolence of her acts of trade and navigation." The Green Mountain area between the Connecticut River and Lake Champlain—present-day Vermont— an area long in dispute between New York and Massachusetts, had set up its own government in 1777, solicited British support of its independence even to the extent of promising neutrality in the Revolutionary War if that independence were recognized, and sought to negotiate a separate treaty of peace with Great Britain. In the 1780s, fearful of being parcellated out to avaricious neighbors, it maintained that it was no part of the United States. Separatism existed in the western areas of Virginia (Kentucky) and North Carolina (Tennessee), territories which had not been surrendered to the Confederation government. With the Appalachian Mountains separating them from the eastern seaboard, the western settlers looked upon the Mississippi River and its tributaries as their "window" to the world. But Spain controlled New Orleans, the lower Mississippi, and the whole west bank of the river, closing it to American traffic in 1784. A complicated series of events led, in the mid-1780s, to both Congress and North Carolina claiming the Tennessee settlements, though neither exercised effective control or afforded the governmental services which the settlers expected. Hence the settlers established themselves as the state of Franklin and, until 1788, alternately asked for admission to Congress as a separate state and recognition by Spain as fully independent. For their part, the Kentucky settlers were sorely divided, some seeking to follow the lead of Franklin and solicit independence under Spanish protection, others working for admission to the Congress.

Above all, however, the Congress could not honor the nation's obligations. The war effort had been financed by paper money and loans, and by the end of the 1780s the Congress had made no effective effort to redeem the former or repay the latter, owing ten million dollars in unpaid interest alone and seeking new loans all the time. Again, the Treaty of Paris had provided that the government would enforce the collectibility of debts owed by Americans to British citizens and halt the persecution of the loyalists in the various states. Congress, without the power to demand compliance, merely advised obedience and the states did as they pleased, although it should be noted that most had repealed their anti-Tory laws by the end of the decade. The failure to live up to the treaty gave the British an excuse for refusing to surrender the border posts along the Canadian frontier and in the west as the treaty demanded, hence British soldiers still manned such forts as Detroit and Michilimackinac and British Indian traders still reaped their harvest of western furs.

As a beggar in the world, the United States had to accept a beggar's portion—meager fare, indeed. Haughty Dame Britain would not deal with her; she did not even condescend to establish a diplomatic legation in the United States, although the Congress had a legation in London. All the ability of John Adams as the American representative could not budge the British government, and in 1788 Adams returned home dejectedly. And France, which had served as midwife at America's birth, thought it best that the infant remain weak and puny. Thomas Jefferson at Paris was almost as helpless as Adams at London, although his reception was far friendlier.

With the difficulties facing the fledgling nation, the American successes abroad and at home during the 1780s were phenomenal. Abroad, the French did open their West Indian islands to American ships on favorable terms. Jefferson was able, at least on paper, to obtain favorable treatment of American vessels in French ports. Commercial treaties were successfully negotiated with the United Netherlands (1782), Sweden (1783), and, although more limited, with Prussia (1784). Morocco, one of the Barbary states, after demanding £ 200,000 in tribute, eventually accepted $10,000 worth of "gifts" and signed a treaty in 1786, although Algiers, Tripoli, Tunis, and even occasionally Morocco still seized American ships. And Spain, although dealing with secessionists in the west, thought it best to reinsure her hold on the Mississippi and sent Don Diego de Gardoqui as an emissary in 1785. In conversations with John Jay, Congress' secretary for foreign affairs, Gardoqui suggested a favorable trade treaty and a stabilization of the vague Florida boundary established at Paris in return for the United States' eschewing the use of the Mississippi for twenty-five years. In terms of the greatest good for the greatest number, agreement along these lines would have been an asset, and Jay saw it as such. So too did a majority of the Congress. But Southern leaders, who would not necessarily benefit, saw the pact as derogatory to the national honor and five Southern states voting against was enough to defeat the treaty.

At home, no part of the nation broke away, although many thought it a distinct probability. "A disunited people till the end of time," an Englishman wrote, "suspicious and distrustful of each other, [the Americans] will divide and subdivide into little commonwealths or principalities ... [with] no center of union and no common interests." State governments were proving viable in their republican guise, albeit political factionalism was running strong and political battles were rancorous. The economy was slowly recovering. Even the Confederation government was working reasonably well at some things. A coinage scheme devised by Jefferson early in the decade was adopted, committing America to the dollar rather than the pound sterling; the various secretaries were building professional staffs which would form the basis of the federal government of the 1790s. And in one area the Confederation government set a lasting pattern.

As a result of the contest over ratification, the Northwest Territory had been ceded to the central government and in a series of ordinances in the 1780s the Congress established the mechanism to effect a wartime promise of 1779 that "unappropriated lands that may be ceded or relinquished" to the government would "be disposed of for the common benefit of the United States and be settled and formed into distinct Republican states, which shall become members of the federal union." (Britain had in essence precipitated revolution by her inability to accept the principle of equality between herself and the parts of the empire; the former colonists were displaying a dedication to the union of equal parts.) In 1784 a first ordinance provided that the territory was to be organized into ten districts within which the settlers were to erect their own governments; when a district's population reached that of the smallest state in the union, it would be admitted into the Congress. In 1785 a second ordinance made provision for the survey of the territory and its division into six-mile-square townships and 640-acre sections, the idea being that as the land was surveyed it would be sold at public auction in section-size tracts.

The ordinance of 1785 established a system for the future, but at the moment it was a fiasco. The survey was not begun until 1787, hence legal settlement was delayed at a time when men were pushing west. Moreover, the system anticipated a minimum sale of 640 acres for $640, the minimum bid in the ordinance being $1 an acre—too much land at too high a price for the average settler.

Hence squatters moved into the territory and all efforts by the 600-man Continental Army to keep them out were unavailing. In 1785 when eastern speculators offered the Congress a lump sum in return for a large, unsurveyed bloc of land, the Congress, perpetually in need of money, accepted, selling one million acres to an "Ohio Company" organized by New England ex-Army officers and five and a half million to a "Scioto Company." Not only did the Congress set aside its own ordinance, but it accepted seventy-five cents an acre in depreciated paper money; in hard-money terms it received eight cents an acre for the land. The presence of squatters and speculators in the territory caused a revamping of the governmental system established in 1784, Congress passing a third ordinance in 1787. No longer would the settlers, from the very beginning, have self-government. Instead, Congress imposed an appointed governor, secretary, and three judges on the territory, although providing that when the population reached 5,000 a general assembly would assume legislative functions. Sixty thousand people would entitle any portion of the territory to establish its own constitution and apply for admission as a co-equal state, but not more than five states were to be established in the territory. This final ordinance set the pattern by which virtually every new state was to enter the union.

Toward a More Perfect Union

The nation as it took form in the years of war and the early '80s was the fabrication of the political leaders who had inspired the Revolution. Their loyalty, political activity, even republican vision had been confined to their states, and the loose union of sovereign provinces under a central government devoid of power in the local sphere embodied their view of the old empire in its pristine, pre-1763 form. Men like Patrick Henry and Sam Adams, firebrands of the '60s, were satisfied.

Yet there were, very early, those who were dissatisfied —men whose revolutionary careers had been closely tied to the nation as those of Henry and Adams—state leaders during the war—had not been: George Washington, who had commanded the rebel army; Robert Morris, sometimes called the "financier" of the Revolution because of his financial activities on behalf of the Continental Congress; John Jay, a delegate from New York to the First and Second Congresses, president of the Congress in 1779, a diplomat abroad in the early 1780s, and the Confederation's secretary for foreign affairs from 1784. And particularly there were younger men who had been involved in the Revolution but at such an age as to catch its ardor without understanding its origins—Alexander Hamilton, for example, a boy of eight on the British West Indian island of Nevis when the Stamp Act was passed, and an *enfant terrible* of eighteen when, as a student at King's College, New York (Columbia University), he entered into the pamphlet warfare of the "intolerable act" days with *A Full Vindication of the Measures of Congress from the Calumnies of Their Enemies*; James Madison, seventeen in 1769, just beginning his studies at the College of New Jersey (Princeton), at twenty-three entering political life as a member of the Orange County, Virginia, Committee of Safety of which his father was chairman, and at twenty-five a delegate to the Virginia Convention which framed the state's first constitution. Such men had a commitment to the nation as a whole, one born in their participation in the Revolution. Young men in a hurry, they had a vision of national grandeur and were not content with the slow progress of the 1780s. Congress' financial insolvency and inability to act with decision, the disrepute of the United States abroad, Britain's retention of the border posts— these things grated upon them and from early in the decade they sought change, reform, a strengthening of the central government.

The nationalists or, as Hamilton phrased it, those who were thinking "continentally," were a small band of ardent, like-minded men. They have been described as "plotters," yet that is to imply a unity and concertedness

which as a group they did not have. And their individual
dissatisfaction was difficult to transform into concerted action; inertia, if nothing else, stood in the way. They grum-
bled and worked for change in small and diverse ways
through the Congress and in their states. In the end it was
less their activity and more the emergence of a broader
desire for change among political leaders which brought
the change about.

This desire for change stemmed from pressures mul-
tifarious and complex, some precise and real, others vague
and merely in the minds of men. There was, to an extent,
a feeling born in a concern for the welfare of a particular
state that there were things which nothing other than a
stronger national government could do to alleviate conditions and speed prosperity within the state. Thus in 1785,
the Massachusetts legislators, their state groaning under a
heavy tax burden, the commerce of their merchant-con-
stituents improved but still depressed, voted a proposal to
strengthen the central government. That same year a
proposal to allow the Congress the power to establish an
impost both for revenue purposes and as a counter in the
international game of give and take was defeated only by
the negative vote of New York.

More basically, however, men of substance and standing
everywhere were vaguely uncomfortable as they sensed
new attitudes and expectations in their states. They had
brought with them from the colonial period a feeling that
respect, deference, and political authority were their
proper due. Their republicanism encompassed this feeling: The end of government was properly the public good
and government must emerge from and be responsible to
the people. However, those who governed ought properly
to be men of substance and standing, free to apply their
reason and knowledge to the determination of what was
for the good of the public.

All about them, however, men of substance and standing
discerned challenges to these propositions. The war and
the economic readjustments required by the departure

from the empire offered opportunities for new men to rise in terms of wealth. The readjustments of political life as royal governments gave way to republican governments— the simple increase in the number of offices to be filled by former colonials with the ouster of empire officials and the departure of the Loyalists who had held offices—gave opportunity for men to rise in terms of power. Men of long standing position in their communities sensed challenges from men newly risen or in the process of rising, "the scum which was thrown upon the surface by the fermentation of war," Pennsylvania's Benjamin Rush called them in 1786. Men of substance and standing sensed, too, that men of *neither* substance *nor* standing—ordinary men— were entering the political arena to demand the fulfillment of their particular hopes and aspirations from governments extolled in press and pamphlets as governments based upon the people. The real extent of the threat to established leaders is debatable but in a sense irrelevant. Even the least threat engendered at least some sense of insecurity on the part of men once secure in their monopolization of politics. And insecure men, seeking to renew their security, clutched at the notion of change.

Such insecurities in part precipitated and certainly underscored a growing pessimism about the fate of republicanism in America. In states where factional politics were particularly rancorous in the '80s and all factions, as befitting proper republicans, were rhetorically appealing to (and claiming) the support of the people, some leaders were beginning to fear that on the small scale of state politics men lacking virtue—more often than not new men, Rush's "scum"—were perhaps taking advantage of republican forms to forward themselves. They were coming to doubt that the people as a whole, for whom and upon whose strength republics existed, had virtue enough for republicanism. It was a doubt inherent in the prevailing situation of politics and political rhetoric: In the politics of factions which marked the colonial period, royal and proprietary governors awarded and withheld positions of power; in the politics of factions of the new nation, the people, at least in terms of republican rhetoric, determined. A political leader ascribing virtue to himself and a lack of virtue to an opponent inevitably doubted, if he lost, the virtue of a people who had given power to his unvirtuous opponent. And few political leaders won consistently. To men with such doubts, the growing salvation for republicanism seemed to be a redistribution of power between the individual states and a strong federal government removed to some extent from the people.

During the Fall and Winter of 1786 the sentiment for change among America's men of substance and standing was vastly augmented. In western Massachusetts the tax burden and the continuing low prices of agricultural commodities (as a result, of course, of depressed commerce and the low level of agricultural exports) finally proved too much for the rural populace. Farmers convened in county conventions to compile and forward grievances to Boston, then moved out *en masse* to close courts to prevent mortgage foreclosures and judgments for debts and tax delinquency. Governor John Bowdoin called up the militia to disperse the unlawful assemblies and in the confused fighting that followed the "rebels" were downed. Shays' Rebellion as it is called (after one of the farmers' leaders, Daniel Shays, a captain in the Massachusetts line in the Revolution) was of less significance as a rebellion than it was as a catalyst in the minds of political leaders in Massachusetts and elsewhere. To men already insecure and pessimistic about republicanism, the Shaysites exemplified republicanism run to anarchy, their demands—clear assaults upon property—the very opposite of a virtuous sublimation of self, and their violence the antithesis of reason. "Good God, who beside a Tory, or a Briton, could have predicted such a thing," Washington wrote in urging that Confederation troops be sent to the scene. And by subtle mental alchemy, the disturbances in Massachusetts were transmuted in the minds of many into a whole nation tottering on the brink of collapse. Indeed, in September

1787, Elbridge Gerry would speak of his fear "that a civil war may result from the present crisis of the United States" and refer to Massachusetts where "particularly, he saw the danger of this calamitous event."

The vehicle by which change could be effected was already in the making, for all the while national-minded men had been at work. Madison at mid-decade had prompted the Virginia legislature to call a convention to meet in Annapolis, Maryland, in 1786 to consider a national regulation of commerce. And Madison and Hamilton had led the Annapolis Convention to call a second convention to meet in Philadelphia in 1787 to consider general amendment of the Articles of Confederation "to render the constitution of the Federal government adequate to the exigencies of the Union." The Annapolis call had been conveyed to the Congress and by the Congress to the states. It had, consequently, an importance which earlier gatherings (Annapolis itself, for example) did not have. The Shaysite disturbances augmented that importance, and the delegates convened in May 1787 in a solemn mood.

Men who thought continentally were at Philadelphia— Hamilton, Madison, Morris, Washington—and many more who thought only vaguely of the need for change. Yet more important than who was there was who was not. There were still many political leaders who thought no change needed, who stood by the old Articles and the idea of provincial autonomy. Rhode Island, a citadel of provincial thinking, sent no delegates. The Massachusetts legislature passed by Sam Adams in selecting delegates. Patrick Henry "smelt a rat," as he said, and, with Richard Henry Lee, refused to attend even though elected by the Virginia legislature. There were, too, "new men," powerful within particular states, state-oriented as a result, and opposed to change, men whose very rise to power to some extent created the conditions in which the convention met. Governor George Clinton of New York was one such. (To Philip Schuyler of an old established New York family, a leader against Clinton, and a nationalist, Clinton's "family and connections" clearly did not "entitle him to so distinguished a pre-eminence" as New York's governorship.) Clinton sent John Yates and Robert Lansing to represent his negative attitude toward change, but they soon left for home. The result was that one point of view within the nation—that which saw no need for change—was unrepresented. The assembled delegates were committed to change and from the very beginning took up the task not of amending the old Articles but of writing anew.

As the delegates set about the task, the area of agreement among them was large. They were committed to strengthening the central government, giving it at least a revenue independent of the states, the power to regulate commerce, and the ability to deal with foreign powers. They were committed to republicanism, most of them feeling that republicanism could only be preserved by a stronger central government. And, as a result of the debates in their states over the previous decade, the delegates had, in the main, arrived at that political theory which held that the parts of government were properly defined by function—executive, legislative, judicial—and that all parts were properly representative of the people.

Yet old fears and prejudices had not dissipated. Strong central government was still a fearsome thing to most, necessary but somehow to be fenced about so as to preclude tyranny. A powerful executive still posed awesome possibilities, even for such a fervent nationalist as Edmund Randolph of Virginia; when the convention wrote a single president into the constitution, modeling the office after the old royal governors, rather than the three-man executive board he suggested, Randolph pronounced the presidency "a fetus of monarchy" and refused to sign the final document. Province-based prejudices and fears hoary with age cropped up regularly throughout the proceedings: the fear expressed by many that the states would be subsumed entirely within the central government, by small state delegates that their states would be overshadowed by large states, by those of one section of the union that their interests would be dominated by another section. And new fears were in evidence—of a government too subject to popular opinion, of popular attacks on property such as many conceived the Shaysite rebellion to have represented.

Fears and prejudices provoked angry, heated debate, threats of withdrawal, malicious attacks upon the motivation of those of contrary opinion. But the extraordinary feature of the Philadelphia convention was that the delegates could surmount their fears and prejudices, hammering out one practical compromise after another in the interest of "a more perfect union."

By the document that the convention produced, state and central government would share power to a greater extent than hitherto to make of the latter a viable instrument for securing "the common defense, security of liberty, and general welfare" of the whole community of states. Yet the powers of the new central government would be specific, not general:

To lay and collect taxes, duties, imposts and excises, to pay the debts and provide for the common defense and general welfare...

To borrow money...

To regulate commerce with foreign nations, and among the several states, and with the Indian tribes;

To coin money, regulate the value thereof, and of foreign coin, and fix the standard of weights and measures;

To provide for the punishment of counterfeiting...

To establish post offices and post roads;

To promote the progress of science and useful arts...

To define and punish piracies ...

To declare war ...

To raise and support armies ...

To provide and maintain a navy ...

To provide for calling forth the militia to execute the laws of the Union, suppress insurrections and repel invasions ...

To make treaties ... [and] appoint ambassadors, other public ministers and consuls ...

[To admit] new states ...

To dispose of and make all needful rules and regulations respecting the territory or other property belonging to the United States ...

[To exert] judicial power ... [in] all cases, in law and equity, arising under this Constitution, the laws of the United States, and treaties made ... [and] all cases affecting ambassadors, other public ministers and consuls ... cases of admiralty and maritime jurisdiction ... controversies to which the United States shall be a party ... between two or more states, between a state and citizens of another state—between citizens of different states ...

To make all laws which shall be necessary and proper for carrying into execution the foregoing powers.

The exercise of these powers would not be concentrated in one man or body. Rather, power would be divided among the federal executive, legislature, and judiciary, each with a power to check and balance the others. The legislature would consist of two bodies rather than the old Congress' one, the first (the House of Representatives) to include so many popularly elected delegates from each state according to population, the other (the Senate) to include two delegates per state elected by the state legislatures.

This make-up of the national legislature was the "great compromise" by which a whole series of conflicts among the delegates were resolved: that between small states and large states; that between those who, while committed to republicanism, most distrusted popular elections and those who, out of a commitment to republicanism, would have all aspects of government flow directly "from the legitimate source of all authority," the people; that between the firmest nationalists who, to strengthen the central government, sought to base the entire national government directly upon the people of the states rather than upon state governments, and those who were content to have the central government remain an extension of state government. Nationalists and what can be termed confederationists in the convention compromised again when they agreed that the president would be elected by neither state legislatures nor the people but by a special electoral college. But the nationalists had their way when they separated representatives and senators from the states by providing for federal salaries. And nationalists were successful again in the stipulation that the "constitution and the laws of the United States which shall be made in pursuance thereof, and all treaties made . . . shall be the supreme law of the land."

A series of piecemeal compromises set aside, if they did not resolve, sectional fears: The Congress would legislate commercial regulation by an ordinary majority—the Southern states had solicited an extraordinary majority fearing that their export of staples would be sacrificed by northeastern commercial interests—but Congress would be barred from levying an export duty, and approval of two-thirds of the Senate would be necessary to ratify treaties, most of which, it was expected, would be commercial in nature; only three-fifths of the South's slaves would be counted as the basis for representation and in levying direct taxes; Congress would not pass any law restricting the slave trade for at least twenty years.

Convened on May 25, the convention ended its work on September 17. None of the delegates was completely happy with the document they produced. Hamilton, ardent for extreme centralization, played little part after the adoption of the great compromise, while Madison attempted strenuously to overturn the compromise in the interest of a central government less tied to the states. In the end, although a few refused to subscribe, most of the delegates could say with Gouverneur Morris that, "considering the present plan as the best that was to be attained, he should take it with all its faults." Yet their "bundle of compromises," as it has been called and, where compromise was impossible, their ambiguous language—"general welfare," "necessary and proper"—were to serve the nation well. The delegates had managed to sketch a pragmatic system capable of near-infinite interpretation; in future, men would flesh out their sketch, broadening a line left vague here, tempering a too-bold stroke there, utilizing the convention's work as a basis for ever-new ideas born of ever-new situations. The beauty of the document framed at Philadelphia lay not in the fact that it was to be the fundamental law of a perfect union but in the fact that men could continue to search for perfection without resort again to fundamentals.

The delegates had exceeded their call by writing the frame of government anew. They exceeded it again when they attached to their work a ratification procedure and dispatched the Constitution to the Congress of the Confederation with the request that it be sent on to the states. The old Articles could be amended only by the unanimous consent of the state legislatures—a reflection of the fact that central government under the Articles was considered merely an alliance of sovereign states. The delegates at Philadelphia, to make the point that the new government was to be co-equal to the states, stipulated that ratification proceed directly from the people of the nation through specially elected conventions in the states. And to foreclose the possibility of one or two states blocking ratification by inaction or unfavorable action, they stipulated that a mere nine states acting favorably would be "sufficient for the establishment of this Constitution between the states so ratifying." The Congress debated what to do behind closed doors for ten days, then acceded and sent the Constitution to the states, becoming a party to its own death as Richard Henry Lee—vehemently opposed to the Constitution—ironically noted. And the state legislators acceded to the diminution of their authority in calling for the election of ratifying conventions, although not always without a bitter fight.

In these legislative fights, in the ensuing elections by which delegates were named to the ratifying conventions, and finally in the conventions themselves, the pro-constitution forces were a concerted group with a decided aim —ratification. The initiative was theirs. They could play upon the broad theme that some kind of change in the national government was necessary if republicanism was to survive. They could play, too, upon particular interests —those of northeastern merchants who could envision a stronger central government opening up the British West Indian trade; of Connecticut Yankees and Jerseyites whose farm produce was exported through and taxed by New York and who could see an end to such taxation in the new union; of Georgians who could anticipate federal support against Indians and Spaniards—to name but three broad groups. Those opposed to the Constitution, on the other hand, were disunited, defensive, motivated by fears and prejudices, more often than not the very fears and prejudices which the convention had attempted to resolve by compromise: fears in the South of the North, in small states of large states, in large states of small states acting in concert, of a strong executive, above all of an overly strong central government encroaching upon the prerogatives not only of the states but on the rights of the people. Where, many asked, was the bill of rights specifying the limits beyond which this new government might not go? The advocates of the constitution could point to the division of power between the branches which would prevent any one from misusing power, and to the proscriptions and prescriptions lodged in the constitution—against suspension of *habeas corpus,* bills of attainder, *ex post facto* laws—finally promising that the new government would make amendment to encompass a bill of rights a first order of business.

Printer's ink and rhetorical phrases flowed freely during the few months of controversy, those in favor insisting on the "numerous advantages promised by a well-constructed Union," those against expressing their fears and doubts, both sides claiming to act in and for the interest of the people. In some states old factions crystallized around the single issue of the Constitution—in New York, for example. But in the end the opposition was overborne, not always by force of polite argument. The contest was brief in Delaware, New Jersey, Georgia, and Connecticut where particular circumstances created a generally favorable climate of opinion and doubters were few. In Pennsylvania, opponents were forcibly constrained to sit in their seats in the legislature when their absence would have deprived the legislature of a quorum and hence the ability to call a ratifying convention. In the ensuing election, those in favor bought up the newspapers and prevented those against from putting their doubts and fears before the electorate. The convention voted to ratify on December 12, 1787. In Massachusetts the pro-constitution leaders resorted to political bribery, promising support to the old-line rebel John Hancock in the next gubernatorial election and suggesting that he might be a logical candidate for federal vice-president, perhaps even president if Virginia did not ratify and Washington—the obvious first choice—was not available. Hancock took the bait and swung enough votes so that the convention ratified 187 to 168. In the Spring of 1788 Maryland and South Carolina ratified, while hard-fought campaigns brought New Hampshire (the ninth state) and Virginia into the fold in June. New York's approbation was vital if the new government was to succeed, but that state's ratifying convention was dominated by George Clinton and a majority opposed change. The pro-constitution forces managed to delay balloting, however, hence avoiding a certain negative vote and quick adjournment, then bluffed wavering delegates with news of Virginia's ratification (hurried north by special post riders), the impending isolation of New York from the rest of the states when those ratifying formed a union without her, and a rumor that New York City was preparing to secede to join the new union. By a margin of three votes the New York convention voted to ratify. North Carolina and Rhode Island held out until November 1789 and May 1790 respectively, but with New York's ratification the new union was assured. The old Congress of the Confederation called for national elections and set March 4, 1789 as the date for the inauguration of the new government.

"Queen of the World, and Child of the Skies"

Over a quarter-century had elapsed between the outbreak of the quarrel with Britain and the adoption of the federal Constitution. During these years ordinary men and women went about ordinary tasks, but in the background of their lives—and sometimes in the forefront when armies clashed near their homes and fathers and sons went off to join the battles, or when riot broke out in their counties and towns—was violence and turbulence, and a continuing political debate as to the nature and form of the new nation which was being born. Inevitably the repercussions of events and arguments were far-felt. It is hard for us almost two centuries away to grasp the metamorphosis that Anglo-America underwent in this situation, for the change was in attitudes and values, and while it was precipitated by the great events of the quarter-century, it was not unconnected with the more gradual metamorphosis over the years from 1607 to 1763.

In the tempestuous days of revolution anachronisms were done away with. Thus the last vestiges of feudal land tenures were abolished in favor of alodial tenures. Proprietorships were ended—the Penn family's proprietorship of Pennsylvania, the Baltimores' of Maryland, and lesser ones in Virginia and North Carolina. Quitrents were no longer paid to king or proprietor. Ended, too, in the South were primogeniture (the right of the eldest son to inherit all in the absence of a will to the contrary) and entail (the legal ability to bind one's heirs never to alienate property). The tendency toward secularization was aggravated. One senses this in the substitution of political oratory for sermons on public occasions, in the tendency to make more of political anniversaries (Massacre Day, the Fourth of July) than religious, and in movements to separate the state completely from organized religion.

Moreover, the Revolution accentuated features and trends of the colonial period. The small tendency toward free trade among American merchants was accentuated when, during the Revolution, the rebel colonies threw their ports open to all and sent their ships into previously illegal trades. After the Revolution, the closing by Mother Britain of her West Indian islands led quite naturally to the demand for free entry and free trade as a right due to all humanity. The fluidity of the colonial social structure and of the political structure were reinvigorated as the Revolution opened new opportunities for men to rise economically and politically. The equalitarianism which underlay political and social fluidity, seldom explicitly recognized or enunciated in the pre-revolutionary years, was reinforced by the political dialogue which accompanied the Revolution and accented the equality of man in a natural state, by the bald assertion in the Declaration of Independence that "all men are created equal." The very politics of the new nation, the constant reiteration by battling factions of *the people* as the source of political authority, gave a political connotation to equality, for while those who used such words generally meant "people of property," some of those who read and heard the phrase understood simply "people." And the whole aura of authority, of men of low degree accepting deferentially the rule of men of high degree—an aura challenged in the Awakening—was challenged again in the Revolution. Beyond accentuating such features and trends, the Revolution provoked a national consciousness. The proud Briton of 1763 became a proud American. The transition was not easily accomplished, despite the differences between mother and children which had developed over the years, the existence of a small kernel of American identification during the late colonial period, the common American cause of the Revolution, and the creation of a single American government.

True, the lions and unicorns adorning public buildings, the statues of George III—the physical embodiments of being British—could be quickly and easily torn away. Anglicans could easily scratch out the name of George III in the supplications for the king's health and well-being in their prayer books and insert "the United States of America," interlineations which can still be seen in old copies of the Book of Common Prayer preserved in Virginia. Hierarchic denominations of all sorts could sever their ties with English hierarchies and erect American ones, as the Anglicans did in creating the Protestant Episcopal Church in 1786 and the Catholics in 1789 when Father John Carroll of Baltimore became the first American Catholic bishop. And intellectuals could form their own scientific and philosophic societies rather than solicit election to the Royal Society in London.

But the Americans could do little about customs, manners, and language which betrayed the enduring link to the British parent—although a young Connecticut schoolmaster, Noah Webster, tried, publishing among other books *The American Spelling Book* (giving us an American "labor" rather than British "labour," "wagon" rather than "waggon") and there were even suggestions to adopt Latin, Greek, Hebrew, or an English-Indian compound as a national language and dispense with English altogether. Washington's victorious troopers swinging down from the Highlands to New York in 1783, singing a British ditty,

THE NEW PANTHEON OF HEROES

WASHINGTON

are significant: The Americans had no song of their own, no overt national culture to set themselves automatically apart. Independent, they were nevertheless as they had been—Anglo-Americans.

This absence of an overt uniqueness lies behind the vehemence with which Americans proclaimed their national identity during and after the Revolution and the direction that their boisterous nationalism began taking Basic ideals conceived of as peculiar to themselves, rather than outward peculiarities which they did not have, served as the building blocks of their nationalism. Republicanism became an article of national faith, as did the tendency toward equalitarianism. The simplicity and plenty of an agricultural way of life was cherished. And while political philosophy held that a republic rose or fell on the strength of the virtue of its citizens and some Americans with a bent to political philosophy called forth the virtue of their fellow citizens in support of republicanism, most

Americans, by an adept reversal, proclaimed their virtue as an adjunct of their republicanism rather than as a necessary prerequisite.

Republicanism, the purity and abundancy of a simple agricultural life, a virtuous and free citizenry—these qualities the Americans took as national characteristics. Conversely (and, of course, to uphold themselves as servants of the future and to enhance their peculiarities) they denounced as archaic and outmoded, even sinful, the contrasting characteristics of mother England and her sisters of Europe. Thus, praising America as a republic, they condemned Europe as monarchial. Praising their own tendency to equalitarianism, they condemned aristocracy and the division into classes. (When, in 1783, for example, ex-army officers organized the Society of Cincinnati with hereditary membership, the generality called down anathemas on them and forced dissolution, considering that hereditary membership tended toward aristocracy; even a medical society proposed in Connecticut was denounced, the reasoning being that it was conducive to the erection of medical practitioners as a privileged order.) Praising the simplicity of American life, they condemned the complexities of Europe. Praising the plenitude of American agricultural existence, they condemned the poverty and want of Europe. And praising American virtue, they condemned England and Europe for their vice. Indeed, all aspects of society were evaluated in terms of this contrast, the Americans making a fetish of whatever of Europe they did not have.

Such nationalism was trumpeted in poetry, plays, letters, and political tracts. From prologue to final speech, Royall Tyler's play, *The Contrast* (1787) displays it:

> *Exult each patriot heart!—this night is shown*
> *A piece, which we may fairly call our own;*
> *Where the proud titles of "My Lord! Your Grace!"*
> *To humble Mr. and plain Sir give place.*

So read the first lines of the prologue, while in the course of the play itself the fine gentleman "who has read Chesterfield and received the polish of Europe" is bested by Colonel Manly, "the untraveled American." "Probity, virtue, honor, though they should not have received the polish of Europe, will secure to an honest American the good graces of his fair country-woman, and, I hope, the applause of THE PUBLIC," the staunch colonel announces in his final speech. And Thomas Jefferson, in letters:

No American should come to Europe under 30 years of age; and [he who] does, will lose in science, in virtue, in health and in happiness, for which manners are a poor compensation, were we even to admit the hollow, unmeaning manners of Europe to be preferable to the simplicity and sincerity of our own country. . . .

Behold me at length on the vaunted scene of Europe! . . . I find the general fate of humanity here most deplorable. The truth of Voltaire's observation offers itself perpetually, that every man here must be either the hammer or the anvil . . . the great mass of the people are . . . suffering under the physical and moral oppression. . . . Intrigues of love occupy the younger, and those of ambition the more elderly of the great. . . . Much, very much inferior this to the tranquil permanent felicity with which domestic society in America blesses most of its inhabitants, leaving them to follow steadily those pursuits which health and reason approve, and rendering truly delicious the intervals of these pursuits.

History was tailored to conform to the national image: The first settlers in America had fled from Europe seeking tranquility and the simple life in virgin forests; their story was one of constant struggle against a tyranny reaching out from Europe for them, culminating in the epochal Revolution wherein tyranny in America had been finally and forever overthrown by brave citizen-soldiers. A pantheon of American heroes was erected to replace that of British heroes, with Washington in the place of honor. ("Begin with the infant in his cradle," Noah Webster prefixed to his *American Selection of Lessons in Reading and*

Speaking of 1785; "Let the first word he lisps be Washington.") Republican Greece and Rome, rather than England and Europe, were taken as the historic antecedents and models for the new republic. And conforming to their self-perception as innovators and servants of the future, Americans considered their own place in history in extravagant terms. In their simple, virtuous republicanism was "a new order of the ages," even the final and best form of human society. Poet Timothy Dwight, writing in the late 1770s:

> *Columbia, Columbia, to glory arise,*
> *The queen of the world, and child of the skies!*
> *Thy genius commands thee; with rapture behold,*
> *While ages on ages thy splendors unfold.*
> *Thy reign is the last, and the noblest of time,*
> *Most fruitful thy soil, most inviting thy clime....*
> *To thee, the last refuge of virtue design'd,*
> *Shall fly from all nations the best of mankind;*
> *... earth's little kingdoms before thee shall bow,*
> *While the ensigns of union, in triumph unfurl'd*
> *Hush the tumult of war, and give peace to the world.*

To an extent, the building blocks of this nationalism were firmly lodged in the colonial past. From the very beginning, the image of America had encompassed the notion of the New World as virgin, untouched, a land where men could live in blissful perfection. The utopian idea of a virtuous republic was one in a long succession of utopian dreams, from Sir Thomas More's *Utopia* of 1516 through the dreams of Puritan John Winthrop, Quaker William Penn, and philanthropist James Oglethorpe. And the contrast to virgin America had always been corrupt Europe. The republicanism of the new nation, moreover, rested firmly upon the strength that the representative lower legislative houses had won during the colonial period, and this embryonic republicanism had even before the Revolution prompted a eulogy of virtue, a disdain for

Europe, and a favorable comparison with classic Rome and Greece. The colonial economy had been—and the national economy would be for long—based upon agriculture, and agrarian simplicity, even in the colonial years, had been extolled.

Yet to an extent the national image was basically ahistorical, even irrational—are farmers axiomatically purer than non-farmers? is simplicity axiomatically preferable to complexity? Certainly America was not as simplistic, virtuous, and classless as the national image that was forming presupposed. There had always been a division of society between "the better sort" and the generality, between rulers and ruled; indeed, the events of the 1780s seem to have thrust a consciousness of the distinction upon the better sort as, in reaction to fears and insecurities born of demands from the people, the better sort gravitated toward change and the Constitution. Competition for economic betterment, even wealth and honors, rather than a virtuous sublimation of self to the good of society was (and had generally been) the rule in America, and the awareness of this lack of public virtue, evoking pessimism about republicanism's fate, was at least a part of the motivation of those soliciting change in the 1780s. The colonial (and national) economy was compounded of more than honest, hardworking farmers, self-sustaining on their few acres (and thereby free from the complexities of an inter-dependent economy); agricultural America was always dependent upon a complex commercial apparatus extending from the smallest village through the port cities of the coast to markets overseas.

Certainly, too, the colonial period had encompassed far more than the simple struggle against tyranny which the Americans were extolling. And America was not and never would be free from Europe. As historian Howard Mumford Jones has commented in *O Strange New World* "kicked out of the door, Europe crept back through the window." Poets and pamphleteers might inveigh against European manners and styles which the modish required, but

> ... *all, which aims at splendor and parade*
> *Must come from Europe, and be ready made.*
> *Strange! we should thus our native worth disclaim*
> *And check the progress of our rising fame.*

And try as they might, "the Americans," in Jones' words, "could not invent a new language, a new system of laws, new educational institutions, a new philosophy, and new forms of literature and the arts that would not be tainted with the profligacy and politics they were pleased to attribute to the Old World."

However ahistorical and irrational, the national image became a factor of history, an "event" in and of itself which would have its effects upon other events. The picture of simplistic, virtuous, and classless America and decadent Europe, for example, would dominate American foreign policy for over a century and a half. The most apparent contradictions between image and reality would demand resolution. Thus the equality of man bumptiously proclaimed ran counter to the existence of slavery. Men were uncomfortable in the situation and in the North, where slavery was relatively unimportant as a social and economic factor, the institution was done away with. Slavery persisted in the South, however, furthering a sectional dichotomy which even a civil war would not fully resolve. Similarly, the very enunciation of a national identity and, in the Constitution, of the perfect union of states, ran counter to an abiding provincialism; again, even a civil war would not resolve the dichotomy. Equality, republicanism and the image of a virtuous citizenry ran counter to the existence of degrees within society and to the prevailing ethos which held that political leadership was the obligation and right of men of high degree. In time another ethos would have to develop to complement rather than contrast with the image, one in which a plain, humble birth (or at least the pretense of such) would be a political asset. Above all, however, the image of republicanism, with its exaltation of a government derived from and responsible to the people—*all the people*—would, by its assumption of a singular and homogenous people, cloud the fact that America was a land of peoples. It is no accident that one writes of the making of a national image during the revolutionary years in terms of Anglo-America, with no reference, for example, to the German-speaking Pennsylvanian or to the black. The image evolved without reference to them. In the years beyond 1789, governments drawn from but one of America's people—the White, Anglo-Saxon, Protestant and propertied—would claim that being of the people and elected by the people, they ruled for the people. One after another of America's peoples—the propertyless laboring man, the immigrant, the Catholic, the Jew, the non-white, the impoverished—would rise to claim it was not so.

But this is to stride forward into the national period of American history. With the emergence of a national image, the first period of our history—the morning of America—comes to a close.

A Short Note on
Further Reading

THE LITERATURE OF the colonial and revolutionary years of American history is enormous and, in terms of shifting interpretations, complex. Various essays in Ray Allen Billington, ed., *The Reinterpretation of Early American History* (1966) can serve as admirable introductions to this literature, particularly the essays of Edmund S. Morgan (on "The Historians of Early New England"), Frederick B. Tolles ("The Historians of the Middle Colonies"), Clarence L. Ver Steeg ("Historians and the Southern Colonies"), Jack P. Greene ("Changing Interpretations of Early American Politics"), and Douglass G. Adair (" 'Experience Must Be Our Only Guide': History, Democratic Theory, and the United States Constitution"). Ideally, the curious reader—realizing that history is constantly being rewritten—will utilize such historiographical essays not only to find particular volumes on subjects which are of interest to him, but to place the volumes he does find within the context of shifting interpretations. Here, for the immediately curious, I offer a short, highly select group of titles chosen for their readability as well as their scope and interpretation.

Peter Laslett's *The World We Have Lost* (1965) is a marvelous introduction to the pre-industrial western world in which the American colonies had their beginning and within which they developed; when combined with J. H. Hexter's "Personal Retrospect and Postscript" (in his *Reappraisals in History: New Views on History and Society in Early Modern Europe* [1961]), Laslett can offer a way of approaching this pre-industrial world far different from that of most historians.

Franklin T. McCann's *English Discovery of America to 1585* (1952), A. L. Rowse, *The Elizabethans and America* (1959), and (although flawed in some ways) Louis B. Wright's *The Dream of Prosperity in Colonial America* (1965) sketch the basic data with which one can reconstruct the unfolding image of the New World as it appealed to Carl Bridenbaugh's *Vexed and Troubled Englishmen, 1590–1642* (1968).

One is best introduced to the founding and development of the Southern colonies through Wesley Frank Craven's *The Southern Colonies in the Seventeenth Century, 1607–1689* (1949), the first of a multi-volume *History of the South* under the editorship of Wendell Holmes Stephenson and E. Merton Coulter; volume II on *The Southern Colonies in the Eighteenth Century,* by Clarence L. Ver Steeg, is forthcoming. Note, too, Carl Bridenbaugh's *Myths & Realities: Societies of the Colonial South* (1952) and Arthur Pierce Middleton's *Tobacco Coast: A Maritime History of Chesapeake Bay in the Colonial Era* (1953). No other region, however, is so fortunate from the standpoint of the availability of concise, general studies of cultural growth and events. New England studies have, during the past few decades, been conjoined with "Puritan" studies, particularly in the many works of Perry Miller. Two of his works stand out: *The New England Mind: The Seventeenth Century* (1939)—a difficult book for those unused to the domain of pure ideas—and the more narrative and readable *The New England Mind: From Colony to Province* (1953). Only recently have attempts been made to consider the development of a New England culture apart from but encompassing Puritan culture, most notably in studies of specific New England communities. Sumner Chilton Powell's Pulitzer Prize-winning *Puritan Village: The Formation of a New England Town* (1963) and Kenneth A. Lockridge's *A New England Town: The First Hundred Years* (1970) are examples. Most of the present author's work has been of this sort, notably *Winthrop's Boston: Portrait of a Puritan Town, 1630–1649* (1965) and *American Puritanism: Faith and Practice* (1970). The "Middle colonies" are almost devoid of regional consideration, for it is debatable whether the colonies from New York to Delaware had enough in common to warrant regional consideration. Thomas Jefferson Wertenbaker's *The Founding of American Civilization: The Middle Colonies* (1938) is a valiant attempt.

A particularly good study of all the colonies during a vital but little understood period is Wesley Frank Craven's *The Colonies in Transition: 1660–1713* (1968). Narrower, but highly suggestive, are the introductory essays in Michael G. Hall, *et al.*, eds., *The Glorious Revolution in America* (1964).

On particular subjects self-evident by virtue of titles, note: E. A. J. Johnson, *American Economic Thought in the Seventeenth Century* (1932); pertinent chapters of volume I of Joseph Dorfman's *The Economic Mind in American Civilization* (1946); Stuart Bruchey, *The Roots of American Economic Growth, 1607–1861* (1965)—containing much on the period to 1789; Bernard Bailyn, *The New England Merchants in the Seventeenth Century* (1955); and his *Education in the Forming of American Society* (1960); Carl Bridenbaugh, *The Colonial Craftsman* (1950); Darrett B. Rutman, *Husbandmen of Plymouth: Farms and Villages of the Old Colony, 1620–1692* (1967); Abbot Emerson Smith, *Colonists in Bondage: White Servitude and Convict Labor in America, 1607-1776* (1947); Winthrop D. Jordan, *White over Black: American Attitudes toward the Negro, 1550–1812* (1968); Edmund S. Morgan, *Virginians at Home: Family Life in the Eighteenth Century* (1952); Alan Heimert, *Religion and the American Mind from the Great Awakening to the Revolution* (1966) —a work to be tempered by the suggestion of a secular basis for religious revivalism contained in Richard L. Bushman, *From Puritan to Yankee: Character and the Social Order in Connecticut, 1690–1765* (1967). Two books are revealing of the nature and dynamics of political institutions: Charles S. Sydnor, *Gentlemen Freeholders: Political Practices in Washington's Virginia* (1952) and Jack P. Greene, *The Quest for Power: The Lower Houses of Assembly in the Southern Royal Colonies, 1689–1776* (1963).

From different vantage points—one colonial society, the other the empire—Charles M. Andrews' *The Colonial Background of the American Revolution* (1931) and Michael G. Kammen's *Empire and Interest: The Politics of Mercantilism and the First British Empire, 1660–1800* (1969) sketch broadly and concisely the situation within which the Revolution occurred. Other studies successively narrow the focus: Esmond Wright's *Fabric of Freedom, 1763–1800* (1961); Edmund S. Morgan's *Birth of the Republic, 1763–1789* (1956); Eric Robson's *The American Revolution in Its Political and Military Aspects, 1763–1783* (1955); Bernhard Knollenberg's *Origins of the American Revolution, 1759–1766* (1956); Edmund S. and Helen M. Morgan's *The Stamp Act Crisis: Prologue to Revolution* (1953)—for many historians the crucial crisis. But the whole aura of the Revolution is (in the light of current work) inexplicable without recourse to the political theories and imagery of the eighteenth century. And in this regard see Lawrence H. Leder's *Liberty and Authority: Early American Political Ideology, 1689-1763* (1968); Bernard Bailyn's *The Origin of American Politics* (1968); his *The Ideological Origins of the American Revolution* (1967); and Gordon S. Wood's *The Creation of the American Republic, 1776–1787* (1969). That the dreams and expectations of republican America which Wood describes in this last were linked to dreams and expectations implicit in the American image in the European mind from the beginning is a point brought home by Howard Mumford Jones' *O Strange New World: American Culture, The Formative Years* (1964).

Index